KENYA

SOME PLACE TO GROW

outskirts
press

Authors Note

Whatever you go through in life, use it as a learning opportunity. Accept the things you can not change. Turn those hardships and battleships into genuine friendships, relationships, and self- ships. Create your own garden of growth. Let go of the pain from the past and embrace the beauty of indifference. Do not allow what you have been through to become of you. Keep pushing until you reach your peace

-Kenya Harris

Table of Contents

About the Author

A Lot of people aren't aware of my story but I finally got the courage to share it because it is very inspirational and could possibly help young girls that may be facing similar challenges I had growing up. My parents were victims of drug abuse leaving my siblings and me terrified of what tomorrow may bring. Who knew it was more to life than Baltimore City and I couldn't imagine ever leaving the hood. Someone had a bigger plan for my life, but bigger wasn't quite better if you aren't pre-pared for change. At times I thought I implemented the right plan for a better life but over time I learned that I had to continue to execute the plan with the little I had. I had many days where hitting rock bottom felt like my days were numbered, but considering everything I've grown from I owed myself a fair shot at life. Entering the system (ward of the state) was the scariest thing I could face alone, my emotions flooded my mind, causing harmful and careless acts. My parents' choices left me to face battles on my own that I was too young to understand, which shaped my reality to react to everything with fear. I struggled for years because I couldn't escape my thoughts and emotions, setting me back from many opportunities. Getting used to change and adapting to new environments created a spiraling frustration inside of me that was waiting to come out. I was blessed with two amazing caregivers that instilled morals, values, discipline, and structure in my life that (wasn't) enough to fight the demon that grew in me. Who would have thought their unbending way of life helped me clean up trails of blood that I would be responsible for?

At times I felt myself using everyone and everything around me to fill voids. I tried to figure out who I was, hoping I'd get far, but God kept setting me back to repeat every task until I learned my lesson. Realizing that God had a plan for my life and the control I fought so hard for was no match. I was facing a battle within myself the whole time. I used drugs, sex, and hatred to numb the pains . I was missing something and I was eager to find out just what it was. I became a lost soul for years until I allowed God to enter my mind, body, and soul to rebuild and reverse the love I thought i lost. I was so tired of fighting myself but life started to look up as I stepped into adulthood. I challenged my emotions which took some work. I learned to feed my soul with positive vitamins. Generational curses became easy to break. I didn't know who I was for a long time so things that I'd done in the past kept resurfacing. I grew to accept my circumstances, forgive my parents, rebuild relationships and work on my inner self which eventually led to healing. Realizing I wasn't missing anything but the peace that God had planted within me. Finding peace made me love myself wholeheartedly. Things started coming together and falling apart at the same time, only this time I wasn't as lost as I was, I found the will of God to help me through anything that came my way.

Chapter 1

In a world full of endless possibilities growing up in the early 90s in what was considered lower class made me question if the odds were against me from birth. In my community you saw struggling families that lived off welfare,you saw the product of the struggling families which were their offsprings . Some were innocent running around en- joying play however they can and some struggled with trauma due to their family circumstances . They were the hustlers, they did anything to survive. They were the ones that lost all hope but created their own and called it living. Last you had the bent over half dead zombies that walked around looking for something to fix their lives, they turned to drug abuse to make their circumstances seem better. With all this going on in my community we were just poor ol helpless kids that wanted to enjoy life as a gift. There was no trees nor grass insight and if you did see soil it was in an old tire with flowers that a generous old lady planted to bring something beautiful to the neighborhood. We had parks but we had to walk a few miles to get there and that was a trip too organized and timely to make happen, so that rarely hap- pened. We had a liquor store on the corner and a telephone booth that everyones used next to it . We had a community center right next door to our home but it was rarely open. Many of the working parents worked long hours so when they came home you would see them go straight in to prepare dinner. Sometimes i knew what was on the menu because i could smell the dinner from their windows. The houses were row homes and the block was so small we had no choice but to smell it. We had plenty of space to run because we didn't have cars parked on the street to take up space. We took up space on public transportation but my family walked most of the time which was better than being packed like a saudine on the bus. For what it was worth my neighborhood seemed pretty decent but even i knew jumping on filthy mattresses in an alley wasn't ideal for any kid. Then there was my family. My parents were victims of drug abuse. Yes they were zombies! at times but they were functioning together which made them the best zombies a child could have. It all started like any other family, I was born into a family of love. I won't take that away from them. At times things made sense, and at times they didn't. I was very young so I didn't quite grasp the way things work. All I knew was if an adult gave an order I was sure to follow it, and if the rules were broken the belt wasn't far away. I can't remember a time where I was actually in two parent home and had what Americans label as a normal life. As the days went on, overnights at my aunt's house became a permanent home for my siblings and i which wasn't so bad at first. In my eyes, my aunt was this superhero. My mom or dad wasn't stable enough to take care of my siblings and me so my aunt stepped up and did the job. She was in her early twenties raising her only child then added her sister's kids to the picture. Which was five at the time. We were pretty close in age. My oldest brother was the golden child. He was close to perfect in my family's eyes. He was silly, cool, and athletic. He didn't bother a soul. He was the protector and man of the house. Then you had the devil child. My second oldest brother. The rebellious one. Hot-headed and ready to fight anyone that looked at him wrong. He was always in trouble. I felt bad for him . I knew it was something deeper than his behavior. Next, There was me the sweet but sassy, intelligent, bossy one. I always tried to keep things in order because I knew what trouble would come if the rules were broken. I was the scared paranoid one. Then you have my innocent, charming twin. He isn't really my twin but we are eleven months apart. We are the same age until my birthday came weeks later. He followed me around but he didn't have so much to say. He just agreed with everything. Last you had the firecracker. The sour one. She was the attitude in the group. She demanded things go her way. I stayed far away from her because she would snap at the blink of an eye. She had a mind of her own. My aunt worked a full-time job at a bank. She was the warmth in my family. Her home was that home that everyone could come to for just about anything. She was a modern day mother Teresa that drank coke forty fives with a bag of plain utz potato chips. I remember holidays like Christmas or Thanksgiving being very special because my aunt made my siblings and I feel as if we were her own. My aunt made sure those days were filled with love. Her cooking was what I honestly think kept us together. As a family we had a hot meal on the dinner table almost every night. Desert was my favorite but if we didn't eat our vegetables we didn't get it. I was always last at the dinner table because i hated peas. I started to smashed them at the bottom of my plate just so i wouldn't have to eat them. Our house was packed so the noise level was what i was immune to. If it was quiet we were punished and couldn't speak a word. If one of us was grounded all of us was grounded. My aunt's daughter was always in charge when my aunt wasn't home. As soon as she left we were animals running wild. The rules went out the window, we just had to make sure we were home by the time she came home from work. The house chores had to be done and everything in place. My aunt was very sweet but if you did something to upset her you would get plucked. She ran a tight home. Every morning for school, she would iron our clothes, lotion our bodies down, and slap petroleum jelly on our faces. She gave us two dollars to get a donut and huggie on our way to school. We walked to school together and we walked home together. I'm pretty sure she could rob a few banks and get away with it, that's how smooth she was. Even though we were living in a time of struggle we honestly couldn't feel if any changes were about to happen. She held everything together. My siblings and I had a pretty consistent and normal routine at my aunt's house.

Chapter 2

Even though things seemed fine I could feel it in my gut that the forecast was about to change. I started to feel the shift in our routine. Some nights dessert wasn't added on the dinner menu,some days my aunt didn't come home,Some nights the thunder kept me up worrying about my parents. I always had questions about their inconsistencies, forgetfulness, and their absence. I saw them often but just like any addiction, it pulls you away from your priorities. How the drug was introduced to them I will never know. I have my opinion of it, but I'm just waiting for that day for them to explain what happened to them. My mom was big on prayers before bed which made me question if she prayed about her condition. I remember one specific birthday I didn't attend school. My aunt woke me up and put my hair into nice ponytails. She used hair gel, water, and grease to slick it all together. She used a hard brush that left white marks on your forehead from brushing so hard. She ironed my clothes afterward and lotioned my legs, arms, and she never forgot my knees. We took a bus downtown to a local Mcdonalds. When my siblings and I got McDonald's it was a reward so I knew this day would be special. It was my birthday and despite all of the circumstances around me that I didn't understand, I soaked up every moment of it. As a gift, my aunt gave me this gold necklace that I didn't want to take off ever. I knew it cost a pretty penny after my mom got a hold of it. She took it and pawned it for her own personal plea-sures. I never wanted to take it off because it was special to me, but my mom was just as special too. After that day it was back to walking to school with my cousins and siblings, coming home doing homework, and running outside until the street lights came on. Some days my mom would show up, but even that stopped. Her lack of support shat-tered every secure bone in my body. Some days I would see her in passing, I would hide behind anything or put my head down so she couldn't recognize me. I eventually just watched her walk pass me be-cause she was in zombie mode a lot. I was too young to understand why it was that way, but as long as I saw her face at times or even randomly popping up to sleep next to me some nights was fine. when she had nowhere to go,she always made her way in my bed. I thought I was okay, but the agony of thinking if she was okay killed me. I would ask myself what kid needed their mother and father anyway when they had just as many people around them that showed just as much love,but that was me trying to convince myself that things would be alright. I remember one night my aunt worked overnight and we were home alone. The lights were out and we all were afraid. My two older broth-ers decided that we would go to his Godfather's house, only three blocks from our house. Seeing them take charge made me appreciate them as men, so taking care of themselves was one less task I had to take on. We walked up the hill very late at night. I had on a long over-size shirt that didn't belong to me and old tennis shoes. I was very tired and so confused. Once we arrived his Godfather welcomed us, but you could almost hear what he was thinking. He shared his bed with all 4 of us. I laid there looking at the ceiling lying in between him and my brothers wasn't the definition of a goodnight sleep. We were so tired from the walk. I tried my best to let go of my worries and what I felt was an uncomfortable situation . Eventually, I fell asleep, but in the middle of the night I woke up because I felt someone hand going up my shirt and trying to pull down my underwear from behind. I did not move because I was so afraid. I slowly opened my eyes to see if my brothers were awake in front of me, but they were snoring like they hadn't slept in days. I thought to myself I have to get out of this uncomfortable space. I got up before anything else could happen. I pretended like I was waking up. I stood by the window all night until I saw the sunrise. My legs grew restless and my eyes were so heavy. I got back into the bed, but this time I buried myself in my brother's arms. My brothers woke up when the morning came and we walked back down the hill together. I never spoke of the incident again. When I would see the monster at a family function I would stare dead in his face with disgust. From that day I knew I had to take control. I would boss my brothers around. It didn't work all the time, but I couldn't let anyone ever take advantage of me again. I noticed that I became defensive but was still soft as cotton. Fear was actually on my side that night. Could fear possibly have a sister? Yes in fact she did, three of them. Faith, courage, and hope! The next time my brothers and I faced hardship I was sure to be the captain or at least a sidekick. Another day came and we didn't have food in the refrigerator. I felt my aunt had given up on us. This was my opportunity to take charge. I started to look in every cabinet. I watched my cousin make pancakes so I attempted to make them. That didn't work out and i wasn't too happy. I'm a master at making them now because I read the box. After all these years, who knew that reading could make circumstances better. I knew my siblings loved pancakes so I continued to try but kept burning them. So in place of the pancakes, some days were jelly sandwiches or my favorite, sweet canned corn. Some days I would take the couch pillows apart or search for coins in every pants pocket we had in the house. The dirty clothes is where I found most of the money. I would get a slice of pizza from Jay Jays to share with my younger siblings. Some days I would eat the slice alone as a reward. I started to go harder for my younger siblings more than anyone else did. My older brothers were more independent. Some days we saw our parents and some days we didn't. When we saw them it was brief, just a simple I love you. Not are you alright or Do you need anything. Months went by and I saw my mother again, but this time she looked very happy and pretty. She even made sense of her words. The first of the month came around and my mother would pop up and take us to Payless to get new shoes. Sometimes I didn't think we would get through the hard times because they started to come to often. We attended church with my Aunt on holidays like Easter, but some days I would walk around the corner to the church by myself. Sometimes I dragged my younger brother along. The pastor was very nice and did not judge or ask questions. I didn't pay attention to the church sermon. I think I just attended for the music and the friendly members. My mom started to come around alot more. She either needed something or just wanted to tell us she loved us. I believed her words but I just wanted her actions to match. I wanted her to be okay in this crazy world. I wanted to save her but even Oprah couldn't save Whitney. I say that to say the most influential, loving, person couldn't save someone that chose that state of mind to block out the world. I like attending school. That was honestly my safe place. My school had many festivities that required support, but no one in my family couldn't afford to take off from their jobs unless it was graduation day. My support was always my siblings and my aunt's daughter. I was satisfied with that. At times i had to be my own support. Halloween we had to dress up for a school parade. My mom promised me that she would get me a costume for the class. The day came and she didn't show up. That feeling of being let down made me feel a feeling I wasn't used to. I sucked up being let down and found a solution. I picked a character that was easy to create with clothing I had. My favorite show was Rugrats . I chose angelica. I put two pigtails in my hair, I grabbed a shirt dress and a pair of leggings and I went to school. I was humiliated because everyone else had parents to buy them real costumes, but I made the best of it for myself without complaining. Graduation came and I remember practicing this song by R. Kelly "I believe I could fly." I sang that song like my life depended on it. I wanted to fly away from the struggle and return with fresh water, food, and money just to create those good days again for my family. I always caught myself daydreaming to block out the reality of things. Windows were my favorite. I always found a window to gaze out of. I felt safer behind the glass creating a vision of what I wanted my own world to look like. As things turned for the worse so did our behaviors. We went from nice and innocent to rebellious and charged.

Chapter 3

We had hiccup days like any other family in the neighborhood. Even though the electricity was turned off and there was no food to eat at times,I knew my aunt tried her very best. My aunt was a hard-working woman. She worked her butt off to make sure all my siblings and her own were cared for. Looking back I honestly don't see how she managed. I would have kicked everyone out, but her heart was pure. Her mother, my grandmother, created a beast when she made my aunt. Rest her soul! My aunt was in her twenties raising her kid and her sister's children on her own. Sometimes I try to imagine how she was feeling. Some days I know she wanted to just give up. She didn't have any time to do things she wanted to do, her life wasn't her own. Her life revolved around us. Today I couldn't imagine raising more than one child. I have one child of my own and that's even a lot. I take as many breaks as needed and I am perfectly fine with it. It takes a village to raise a child, not just a woman.

There were days we had random knocks at the door. We stayed quiet because we knew it was the people. Taking us away from our family was modern day slavery. When I say people I'm referring to Child protective Services. We were aware of these people because we actually witnessed a family being separated in the neighborhood. The noise level in our home wasn't the same. Happy kids made noise. This time the adults made the noise. I heard a lot of commotion downstairs about random people popping up at our home to speak with my aunt, but we ignored them. They were yelling and arguing about our lights being illegally cut on. We had rough days like any other family in the neighborhood, but taking us away would be just wrong. Better days came at least i thought but worse days stayed. The attempt day came and we scattered like roaches when the lights were cut on. This time they entered our home. We hid in the dresser drawers, closets and under the beds for about twenty minutes. My heart was racing. They didn't take us that day, but I knew for sure they would come again. Our household was falling apart and I had no control this time. That day came again for sure, you would think we were illegal immigrants in the country the way the attention was on us as they took us. So many tears, so much screaming. I just wanted whatever was going to happen to us to just happen already. I was too young to fully understand but I watched everything and saw everyone's faces. I thought to myself as we were leaving my aunt's house, could this be what I sang so hard for? I didn't want to fly away. I was sure I was the blame. I didn't want to believe life could get this bad for me, but this was my reality. I wish it was a dream that I was soon to wake from. I closed my eyes and opened them again. I was still in the car leaving my loved ones. We were forced to get in stranger's cars. One of my brothers took off running and never looked back. He was the rebellious one so I didn't expect anything more. We all looked at one another and nodded with our heads, that was our way of agreeing that we would see one another again.

Chapter 4

We drove about 30 minutes away from our home. I stared out the window but this time i couldn't focus. I became nauseous. The car ride was new for me because we usually walked everywhere. I didn't speak a word and neither did my siblings. The worker did not speak a word either. I had so many thoughts going through my mind but I didn't know how to express them. I didn't know what questions to ask. Tears were just dropping in my lap as we drove away. So many feelings built up in my body. I became angry at myself because this was another opportunity to take charge and i didnt. I wasn't a disrespectful child and I wasn't taught to disrespect adults. I sat there and cried. All those superhero shows I watched before school were pointless. My confidence went right out the window. All hope was lost. We finally arrived at this huge house with green grass and huge trees everywhere. The house was very big with a backyard and a playground. Back home in the city, we had one tree on the block and barely a backyard, we had alleys with trash and old mattresses to jump on. We made our basketball hoops out of crates and old wood we found. It was fun and adventurous because we didn't know any better. Here it was like I was in another world,Something you saw on television. A better world here, but not the world I wanted or knew. My older brother went to another home elsewhere. In my mind, I was praying he was alright. We were introduced to even more strangers at the door. It's like they knew we were coming. I couldn't believe strangers allowed other people's kids inside their home. We were introduced to someone else's mother. I called her Ms. C. She was a foster parent. I knew this change would take some getting used to, but some nights I would have silent cries to myself because I missed that feeling of togetherness. I missed the feeling of going to sleep and waking up to my own dysfunctional family.

Three of my siblings were in Ms. C's home with me. I had their back by all means, well not really I was all bark no bite. I would try to get them to do the right things so the wrong things wouldn't happen to us. They had their own mind so they had to accept their own consequences. I was the second oldest there, well I felt like the oldest because once my big brother got caught he eventually came there as well. My big brother was irresponsible and reckless and didn't think rational at all. It wasn't his fault though, With him I always questioned if his acting out was just pain. I wish I could have gone back to ask them how they were feeling about the changes, but I didn't. I swept everything under the rug and kept going on with life. I didn't have a voice anymore and I didn't want to be responsible for their feelings because I had a ton of my own. Ms. C had a playground in the backyard and a lot of space to run free.

Months went by and we developed a consistent routine and schedule. The routine was pretty basic, but the rapport was off. It was no type of family bond whatsoever. I was detached from her and it was hard to fake it. We made some friends, but I was cautious and paranoid about everything. I knew the friendships wouldn't last so I enjoyed every moment. Being there began to feel a little comfortable but it wasn't my family. Ms. C was stern and holy and put us to work. She would make us shuck barrels of corn for dinner. She had rules and locked up everything. I felt like I was in prison at times. This was my new life and I had no choice but to accept it. We had chores like any other kids. We had all the necessities we needed, but we were missing blood. I was still afraid to speak. I would say two words and keep the rest floating in my head, they were safer there. I didn't trust these people. It was her and her daughter in the home. Her home was opened to many kids. I eventually started to loosen up, but not as myself. They didn't deserve seeing the real me, so I gave them what they expected. School took some adjusting, we attended the same school. Meeting new kids and teachers was so terrifying. Just when things seemed ok, it was like trouble began to follow us. We were leaving school one afternoon and a kid was picking on my brother. He called him all types of names. I was sure he had gotten himself in some trouble earlier that day, but we were getting the aftermath of his mess. My other siblings and I sat there to see what would happen. The kid made fun of him because he couldn't spell the word butt. I wanted to yell out, "You get your butt whooped because you are hard-headed." Even I could spell that word, but my brother spelled it "bee-you-tee." I corrected him, but I could feel how humiliated he was. Being absent some days from school back home put us behind. A lot of things I didn't know made me frustrated. I would take my anger out on teachers as if they knew what was going on with me. If our teachers would have known our circumstances I feel like they would have understood us. The teachers weren't getting paid enough to teach kids and deal with personal issues. Days after that incident my brother started to act out alot and Ms. C couldn't handle it. Weeks after that he was removed from her home. I cried so much being in someone else's world I couldn't cry anymore. I knew for sure I would see him again. What state of mind he would be in was unanswered. One thing I realized growing up is that this world will change you if you're not strong enough to fight against it.

It was me, my brother, and my little sister left at Ms. C's home.

My brother and I are eleven months apart. We were very close. I would tell people he was my twin because we were inseparable, and I honestly think we looked just like. Certain things about the way Ms. C did things in her home made me feel trapped. We had a key to C's basement door to get in after school. Behind the door was a room with toys in it and a table to complete our homework. There was a door that leads to the house, which was locked until she got home from work. We had hours to spare until she got home. She would leave us a snack to hold us over until dinner. We would play school or sing random songs. We both loved to sing random old songs, our loud singing eventually turned into crying. Her rules were harsh, but how could we learn if we didn't make mistakes? It's like she just put all of our problems in one room to grow. We weren't prisoners or monsters, we were kids. Harmless and hurt. As i grew i got used to her cold-hearted ways. As I look back, she honestly didn't know how to properly care for kids that were overly emotional. I grew to hate my mom because I needed her.

We needed her. She was miles away and the little hope I had left for her seemed to be leaving as well. Playing for us often turned into real emotions at a very young age and I couldn't control it. My little sister and I were opposites. She was a torch and no one could put her flames out. She was younger, but even I knew not to mess with her. We were settled into C's house but even I knew this wouldn't last. This couldn't be my life. I prayed like my mother taught me for better days. I prayed very hard and very long some days. One day we got a visit from our worker and he explained that the court granted family visits with my mom. I had mixed emotions. The worker was the only source I had to my family, but even he took a long time to come to see us. I started to grow very rude feelings towards workers and lawyers. I turned my face up to anyone that had an opinion about what they thought I was going through or opinions about my family. Every time I met with these people they did a lot of writing. None of those words on the paper could change the family I was born into. Seeing my mothers face for the first time in a very long time made me so weak for her. I ran up to her and gave her the biggest hug. I couldn't get my words out. I had so many questions but all i really wanted to know was when was i coming home. We met in a small room that was kid-friendly. Sometimes the visits were supervised, and other times they weren't. We didn't have a lot of time with her, but we would always tell my mom we wanted to be with her. My siblings were smothering every visit. I finally started to ask questions because I wanted clarity. My heart broke more and more because time was flying and we weren't home. I had to fend for myself in so many ways as a young girl. It was unbelievable! I had to do my hair on my own which wasn't hard because I remembered everything my aunt did. Sometimes C would make me do all the girls' hair in the home. I was so patient with my mother but time beat her at her own race. I started to lose hope even more for me and my siblings future. When I needed to clear my mind i would walk for miles. There was this very large grassy area with large trees that went on for miles. I would go up there and walk until I was tired and just scream. We attended church very often with Ms. C. There were roughly twenty members. C's father was the pastor. We would randomly have scripture contests. We had to memorize certain scriptures and perform them front and center. Of course, I was determined to win. Psalms twenty three stayed inside my head after that. Eventually it stuck to my heart. I recited it many days to myself. I tried to make sense of how it related to my situation. I was very active at C's church. We had no choice. I sang when I didn't have a singing bone in my body and danced when I didn't think I could do that either. We performed in front of the entire church. I didn't like being the center of attention. My fear of being front and center eventually went away because I performed often. I didn't like the members eyes gazing on me. I felt like they were judging my life. My thoughts got the best of me so I couldn't tell if someone was being genuine or not. I didn't know what to feel about Ms C because she seemed like she didn't want to be bothered at times. She was very standoffish. It was very hard to build a rapport with her because I didn't get that nurturing feeling from her. She had to have some significance about her because she had many roles in the church. One thing I noticed about her was that she told me no often, but allowed my younger brother to do a lot. Ms. C became nicer as she started to see I was very responsible and mature for my age. I didn't have friends I could relate to in the neighborhood because most of them were weird. They were different, but I was too so I gave them a chance. At school I was so afraid to make friends. One day a popular girl at school asked me if i wanted to be a part of her clique. It was about seven of them. I became very close to all of them. Each of them had their own personality. I was a part of something and I was happy. We ate lunch together, hung out at recess together, we told each other who we had a crush on, and we even made up dance routines. Sometimes Ms C would let me go over to my friend's house. She lived and breathed dance. She was very good at it. She was very fortunate. She had the latest everything. She was like a star. I felt like Orphan Annie. I wanted to be a part of her life. I lived through her. Some days I would imagine just dressing up in all her pretty clothes and just being her. We grew close. She became a sister. Her Mother was the sweetest. She invited me everywhere. I went to New York City maybe three times with her. She gave me so much life. I opened up to her. We laughed all day. She was so much fun. Her mom was so nice to me, and I felt it was genuine. This was the first woman I actually trusted. I will never forget this finger method she taught me that helps you meditate. She told me to put hands together and cross all of them except your thumbs. Leave your thumbs parallel and try to rotate them around one another without them touching. I felt she knew my secret, but she didn't treat me any differently. I got in the habit of rotating my thumbs when I became anxious. Traveling with them made me feel like the pain I was feeling was only back home. I started to think that maybe this transition was an opportunity for my siblings and i. I was too young to fully grasp the bigger picture. I had one cool friend a few houses down from ours, she was younger but full of life. She had everything a kid could ask for, but she also had a sassy side. Her family had a huge pool in their backyard. They gave my siblings and I permission to swim in it at any time. I almost drowned one day which scared the living hell out of me, but I kept coming back until I mastered it. I became a daring individual after I learned how to swim. I thought I was a fish. I would dive in head first every time. During the wintertime, we couldn't get in, but spring came and I knew it was almost time for the pool to open. We would see tadpoles and frogs all around the pool. I saw all types of new life in that yard. I was so in touch with nature that I wasn't afraid of anything with more than two legs. I would climb trees and walk in the fields all by myself. I would collect frogs and just listen to the sounds of nature. Some nights I would lay in the grass and watch the stars. I would dig tunnels for worms or make clubhouses out of scraps I found while wandering. I had to be in touch with something because the love I did have was gone. I also felt I was never returning home so i stopped questioning myself about that as well. I just accepted it. My brother and I stuck together often but he made his own friends. Have you ever experienced someone giving you the world and on any day decide they wanted it back ? I felt my whole world was taken away.

Chapter 5

Becoming a ward of the state was traumatizing for me. Just knowing I belonged to the state and not my parents made me sick. I felt like someone's property. The system didn't even know what the system was. A system is built to make things work out for the people. No one ever in the system stops to ask how we felt about all the changes. They had the upper hand on where we were placed, or whether or not we were diagnosed with a mental illness. There were so many unfamiliar faces around asking the same questions over and over. I am almost certain that the system had outdated policies that haven't been revised in years to help families like mine. Even if we were perfectly fine and we showed an inch of anger then medication was needed. I often heard the reason we were removed from my aunt was because we were being neglected and not being taken care of properly. The truth of why we were taken away still is left unsaid. Back home things got pretty bad, but who has perfect days or a perfect family. Many great memories of my family disappeared once the horrible thoughts of not reuniting with them started to flood my brain. Growing up away from my family taught me a lot about what being an adult would be like. I had to learn to be responsible, independent, and selfless. I became responsible, independent, and curious at the same time. It was very strange that I didn't grow any bad feelings towards the women in my life because they showed me strength, but the men I despised. That thought of a man violating me left a bad taste in my mouth for all men. There were times I'm pretty sure my aunt and mom did things they weren't proud of. Im more than certain they would do just about anything to make ends meet. I'm pretty sure having a meal on the dinner table almost every night with several mouths to feed was a struggle, especially doing it alone. As I started to go through life I understood that life hits people in many ways, and as much as I thought I had forgiven my mother, I had actually turned my feelings off. I didn't forgive her. I just suppressed the feelings that I didn't want to face. I mastered hiding the pain of my past and creating new memories. It was times I felt that to survive, I had to do things I wasn't proud of. Certain life lessons I learned were through experience which built my strength. I had to understand that there are two sides to everything, and that's how I had to think; whether it was Good and Evil, or Black and White. I appreciated my aunt so much because even when we didn't have much she made it work. I didn't love her any less because she tried her best and that's what counts. When I was in foster care I honestly tried my hardest to forget the memories of not being with the people that birthed me or family members I love. Some nights I felt sad and I needed those precious memories I kept in a safe place to hold me at night to sleep. My trauma flared when I saw everyone around me with a family. I became very timid and afraid of change. I was so afraid that if I uttered one single word that it would change time. I started to believe I was at fault for all of this. I went back into my silent stage. I became very quiet again. I sat and observed everything around me. You know how they say when one sense is weak the others become stronger? My mouth was closed shut, but my eyesight and hearing were ten times better. I was depressed. I didn't want to try anymore. Things got tough way before we were taken away. It was like a sign from God that change was about to come again. I tried to put everything that I've been through from my childhood in the past but like any piece to a puzzle, they fit. Being fearful of change prepared me for a lot of real-life experiences today. At times being afraid helped me think before I spoke or thought before any actions were made. That mindset was the younger me. That all changed once I was bottled up with so many emotions towards the drastic changes I wasn't prepared for. As much I tried to suppress them I noticed I was picking up some pretty ugly habits. I would turn my bossy attitude into power. I made the younger kids do what i say. They looked up to me and wanted to always be around me. I used that to my advantage and manipulated them. I wasn't sure why i wanted to make them feel my pain i just knew feeling it alone wasn't as fun.

Chapter 6

The social worker that dropped me off gave me contact numbers to contact some of my family members when he would visit. The worker would usually check on me before a specific court date, but they didn't come too often. I had multiple workers. I didn't even care to remember their names. I dreaded going to court. Being in that environment made me very emotional. I was ashamed and surrounded by all these white people that didn't know how I was feeling inside or didn't care to ask. The best part about seeing my worker was being updated on my siblings or my family. There were several times my worker had my hopes up thinking I would go back home, but it was up to my parents. ``Our rights were not taken away'' is what my mother would always tell me when we talked. It was still a possibility to reunite with them, but the possibility was a total loss. My parents had to prove that they could take care of us, so what she said didn't matter to me. I started to let her talk. There was no action at all behind it. It was excuse after excuse. It was up to her to get us back and she knew that. I started to grow negative feelings towards her because she could have gotten some strength from somewhere to get us out of the system, but clearly, she was focused on other things. I called often to check on my family. I would cry half the phone call. I started to block my own family out and fall into a dark place. My cries couldn't get me home so I started to find ways to get my mind off of it. I didn't want to drown in my own sorrow anymore. I wanted to see things in a better light. It became so hard to do but I became stronger doing it. I rode my bike for miles but then slept for hours. Sometimes I would stay at my friend's house past the time I was told. I respected her rules but not her. I loved gospel music. Yolanda Adams or Mary Mary were my favorite artists. I felt like every word they would sing. Each song gave me a better insight on life. I loved R&B as well, but I had to listen to it with earphones in my ear because Ms. C did not allow it. If she had some rhythm and blues in her life maybe she wouldn't be afraid to express herself. I needed someone to talk to, and it wasn't Ms. C nor my friends. I was tired of talking to myself. Ms C felt a change in me. She would always say "things could be worse". What she didn't know was I had become numb, and it was no turning back that from that. Things were already at its worst for me. Whenever I started to lose hope I would receive good news. I felt like it was someone around me protecting me. I didn't know who, what and how they were doing it. I started to be at ease with the situation. I prayed at night for a better attitude towards life. I wasn't one hundred percent happy but I wasn't as angry inside as much. I earned money doing chores. I saved every penny because I wanted things like skates, a new bike, or even hygiene products. I purchased everything with my own money that I saved. It felt good not to worry about certain things while I was living with Ms. C. We didn't do things like family movies nights or game nights. Instead we went to mcdonalds every tuesday for their family night. We would also take long rides to the UTZ factory in Pennsylvania. These were things i think she liked more. Those long rides were pretty therapeutic for me. Listening to gospel music while looking out the window. Random teardrops started falling off my face.

Ms. C started to give me a little more freedom. I was able to attend a skating night with some friends. I had so much fun. I helped some of the younger kids that needed help. A few days went by and my neighbor randomly stopped by C's house. She was intrigued by my helpful gestures at skate night. I had no clue she was watching me. She was curious about what I was interested in. This was the most selfless thing a person could have done for me. I was in love with little Bow Wow at the time so I expressed to her that I liked this specific rap artist. She told me she would get me the newest CD. I could have died when she gave me that CD. I was so happy! The first real-life lesson I learned was about integrity- doing the right thing when no one is looking. Things started to look up for me. One day I was told I could have a day visit with my aunt on my father's side. She was super cool. She had every cereal box you could think of. She had a rabbit and a huge German Shepherd. She had naturally soothing things. I had cousins that showed their love in small ways and that's all I needed. They would do my hair, buy me new clothes, and even take me wherever they went. At times I even tried to get away from the orphan image. I loved going there, but I hated leaving. My worker must have recognized that I needed my family because I started to speak more. I went there almost every other weekend. The cool part about it was my sister started to come as well. She went to another stranger's house but I was happy she was around. We argued like cats and dogs. She was a feisty little girl. Soon the visits to my aunt's house stopped. I didn't question why. I just took life as it came. I became bitter inside because my hopes were gone so fast.

The one thing I enjoyed was my school. It was something I began to love. All my classmates loved school so I had to love it too. I didn't want to be left behind again due to my absences so things I didn't understand I tried my best to get. I was very silly in class because I didn't want anyone to see I was lonely or sad inside. One day Ms. C told me I was going to visit my sister. I was anxious and nervous at the same time. I packed my overnight bag and waited the next day to visit. I needed a break from C and her rules. I know she needed a break from me as well. I would never really open up to her about my feelings. You could feel the distance between us and I was ok with it. Picture day at school were the worst for me. I felt so ugly and I hated seeing myself. I honestly wish I had a voice when I was younger because C could have taught me about self-reflection or even tell me how beautiful I was even if I didn't feel it. Back home my aunt always dressed me up nicely and I actually felt pretty. C did not care as long as the check was written in pretty ink. Maybe she didn't understand her role as a foster mom. She didn't have any kids of her own. Her daughter that she raised was adopted. I was curious to know if she actually ever birthed a child of her own. Angelina Jolie has hundreds of kids and I feel her love for them in just one picture.

Chapter 7

Ms. C signed me up for a therapist. A male therapist at that. I despised men so opening up was a task. I gave it a chance, but he talked so much and I was so uncomfortable. His eye contact would make my eyes cross. When he would talk the stench of his oil would make me nauseous. I couldn't stare into his eyes because it made me think he was just like my brother's Godfather. One session he made me write a letter to my dad. The letter was everything I wanted to say to him. I expressed how hurt I was, and how his absence made it hard for me to understand a male role. The letter wasn't genuine. I just wanted him to take the notes he needed so my sessions would be complete. I sealed the letter and threw it away as I left our session. He gave me some encouraging words that made me realize that everyone isn't out to get me but in fact to help me. I started giving others a chance, my attitude started to become more welcoming towards male adults but I still envied them. For a long time I started to look at the current adults in my life the same as my parents and the people that took us away. At times the adults that were in my life were content with the way things worked for them. They didn't care to actually dig deep and see what children were thinking. The side most humans were afraid to cross. The side of a traumatized child. They weren't trying to understand my pain, I was down looking up, and for me to get way up to their level would take time and hard work. Now lets reverse it. What would it take for them to come down to my level and enter my world. Sometimes I thought everyone forgot I was a human being,I felt like my feelings were not normal. Some days I would ask myself was I wrong for feeling how I feel. The answer was left unanswered. The day came and I went to visit my sister. Only this time the house was even bigger. It was another single-family home but this time the grass was much greener. Could this be a better opportunity for me? I didn't know her caregiver at the time, but when I met her I realized Queen and Ms. C had a lot in common. I felt like the Fresh Prince of Bel-Air when I pulled up. It was so neat inside and everything had a place. I spent some time with my sister, but we never really talked about the elephant in the room. Her life seemed very much different from mine but quite similar. It was so much space in the house as well as light. The blinds were open all over. In my mind, I used to think someone could potentially break-in. There were little to no kids running around in the neighborhood and it was very clean. My sister seemed very happy there. The atmosphere did not choke me out as much as C's place did. My sister's foster mom was very nice but straight forward. She had a big family. She had structure. It was no question in my mind that she was the head chick in charge. You could tell by her demeanor. She had rules for days, but morals for life. I stayed a couple of days. I was sure to stay in line. I liked it here and wanted to stay. I spent time with my sister but we honestly stayed out of each other's way. I didn't know where to start. I had questions for her, but I didn't want to create more damage. The day came to return to C's house. The only good thing about her home was that I had real friends at school and I became attached to them. I returned home. I had so much to share but couldn't. I couldn't share my weekend with my friends because they would have asked so many questions after. A few weeks went by and everything seemed normal. I was in class doing my classwork and the principal asked me to get my belongings for dismissal. I was so confused. I honestly wanted to run like my brother did. I thought the worst. I didn't think it was my last day ever seeing my friends. They didn't know I was leaving them. Leaving without notice was easier than telling them I could be going back with my real family. My social worker was in the office, he greeted me with a fake smile. He told me that I was relocating with my sister. I couldn't believe it. I looked back one more time and I left out of the door quickly. This was the happiest day of my life. I went to C's house to pack the little I had and said my goodbyes. I was so proud of myself because I didn't cry. I thanked C for taking me in, but I wish I could have expressed to her that kids need nurturing even if they aren't your own. I hugged her for the first time and grabbed my bags. I taught myself a lot at C's house which made me outgrow my current living situation. I was eager to see what more life had to offer me. That car ride was the happiest car ride of my life. There were no tears, worries, or fear in my body. I was just happy to be closer to my sister.

Chapter 8

I arrived at Queen's house and I was filled with joy. I had little to nothing to unpack which made me feel like a nomad. She was married with kids. She was invested in her family. She was a balanced individual and I wanted to have that trait. There were rules, chores, praying times, family times, and even quiet time. She had many roles. I called her Queen BEE. She reminded me of a queen bee literally. She cooked, cleaned, and even took care of her husband. She wasn't afraid to get dirty either. What I mean by that was she didn't give out chores that she didn't do. She was always cleaning, she was a clean freak. She made us make our bed every morning. This present day I never leave the room without making my bed. She reminded me of the queens I would read about in my government class. She was stern and didn't take any crap. I liked that about her, but I wanted to see her softer side. I knew it was a story behind her strength. She wasn't afraid to express how she felt and I liked that. Even though some of her words came off strong she wasn't afraid to tell it how it was. I wanted someone to be overt with me even if it hurt my feelings. I didn't like people hiding things from me. I wanted things straight forward. I hated doing chores every day. One night I forgot to do my chores and Queen woke me up out of my sleep to do them. I was so sleepy and angry at the same time. I didn't miss another chore from that day. She did our laundry, cooked every day of the week, and still managed to have a prayer. Seeing her do all these things made me want to be just like her. She made it look so easy, but I'm pretty sure behind closed doors the veil was removed. My little sister was used to this lifestyle and she seemed happy so I didn't complain. We ate like a family which I loved. Every Sunday, Tuesday, and Friday we would attend her church. That got draining because the church was so boring to me. We had family prayer every morning before we went to school. She would use holy oil on our heads. She drew the letter t across my head. I didn't know the significance of it at all. During prayer, I would crack one eye open to see who was playing. Queen had two daughters of her own and two family members she took in as well. I gravitated towards her oldest daughter because she was cool as a fan. She had nice clothes and her hair was always on point. She was rarely home because she had a job, but when she came home I was always around her. She was a teenager and I was a growing teen so I paid attention to her moves. I was more to myself at first. Once I became comfortable, I started to engage with everyone a little more. I was getting older so I knew I had to act my age. I always watched her older daughter because I wanted to learn teenage behaviors. She seemed so free. She had her own job, her own attitude, and her own way of doing things. I didn't know if I wanted to be an angel or the devil's child. I didn't have my own sense of self identity so I became everyone. She was the cool kid for the most part, but when she was in trouble it was pretty bad. Quiet time was more of my time. I developed a habit of writing my feelings down. Those words turned into poems. I loved mixing my feelings into beautiful pieces of poetry. Some days the words I wrote were happy and other days my words seemed hateful. Was I bipolar? I don't think so. I just think I was more in touch with deeper emotions and not the baby emotions teachers usually teach us. My emotions had emotions. My words became stories that I didn't want anyone to know. I shared one of my first poems with queen. I knew i would be in her home for a long time, so i wanted her to get to know me and what i was feeling inside. She loved it. She encouraged me to keep writing because one day it would count. I was very proud of that poem. It gave me hope.

Queen's husband and I didn't have a close relationship at first. I didn't quite understand the role of a male figure in my life since I was violated so young. I wanted to open up more with him, but I was still very uncomfortable. It wasn't fair to him that these feelings didn't leave my mind. He was a great father and husband. We eventually had a talk about how a male is supposed to treat a female. Those talks eased my mind a little. Those talks helped me in future experiences. I wanted to call him dad as our relationship grew stronger, but I just couldn't let my guard down until i was ready. I thought adults were supposed to protect children. That image stayed in my head and every male face was my brothers' Godfather. That's when I knew a forced relationship with him wouldn't work. I was too damaged. I was brief with him and it wasn't fair. He was a hard-working man and a gentleman at the same time. He was sharp with his suits every sunday. He opened every door queen walked into. I watched his every move and took notes. Chivalry isn't dead, it was very much alive. A Lot of our down time was productive at queen's home. We didn't have a television in our rooms. We had a television in the family room and we couldn't watch it until everything was complete like homework or chores. I didn't see much of the outside because we were always busy. If it wasn't doctor appointments it was church or school. We were so busy that I didn't have time to feel a thing. Quiet time helped me collect my thoughts and rejuvenate my mind. I got into a habit of organizing the little I had. I would fold and unfold my clothes. I cleaned every inch of the space that was mine. Queen was strict about us making our beds and being sure that our area was clean. She would say "cleanliness is next to Godliness. " Dinner times were the best for me because her cooking was pretty good. She was from North Carolina and her cooking spoke for it. We all took turns to say how our day was. Queen incorporated God in everything she did or said. That got tiring, but I knew if it got me to where she was she could ramble all day. We didn't go shopping much but hand me downs made me happy. I would get all the clothes that her older daughter couldn't fit anymore. We only went shopping to get items that we needed. I didn't come from a family of lots of money so I appreciated everything someone gave me. I attended a local school right behind our home. I made a few friends at the new school, but I made even more friends at church. After entering the system most of the schools I attended had way more resources and a higher quality of learning. I was " the middle class". The area had less police officers and more libraries. They had less stores and more land. They had a diverse group of students and good education. It was a different world. I felt at times the teachers were very lenient on their kind. The caucasian students. I felt they didn't understand our culture so they couldn't possibly know what we needed. Some of my teachers didn't take the time to learn either. The school had kids of different ethnic backgrounds. I was eager to learn about their way of living. I wanted to know everything I didn't know or understand. I made friends with kids from different cultures. Asking them so many questions was overbearing, but I wanted to know how we could all co exist in this world. I was really angry inside, but I didn't let it show. Some days, well most days silence kept me sane, but then others days i couldn't stop talking. I was proud of myself because even if my moods changed often I never let it hinder my growth and development. I attend school dances. I joined clubs. I ask questions to help me understand things I was unsure of but I didnt get too personal. Building genuine relationships with kids at school was easy but i was afraid of what they would do with everything i kept inside. Some kids were evil and bullies. I stuck to what i knew and that was the asian kids or hispanic kids. I attended Sunday school every Sunday with queen. I was very quiet on Sundays because the church leader would pick random kids to ask questions about God that I didn't know. I knew maybe five scriptures and the books of the bible but that was about it. I developed some insecurities because in the past I was picked on so much back at Ms. C home. I was afraid to speak up at times. I felt my voice didn't matter. Everything I wanted to say would just be floating in my head. I was so shy around new people. But I kept coming back because I had an eye for this one boy who acted so goofy. I know he thought I was a creep because I would just stare and not say a word. I looked forward to attending church. I became closer to the Queen's family which made me adapt to their way of living. The amount of discipline and structure she instilled in her family helped me develop a sense of being. I felt it was ok to shed the angry and scared layers off. I became very silly and open to everything. At home the girls and I would have dance sessions and nights where we would play games together. I was making positive memories and I liked it. We developed a sisterhood. We did one another hair, had fashion shows, Movie night and more. Maybe my new life wasn't so bad after all. One thing I appreciated at the Queen's house was pictures. I rarely had any pictures of me or my family growing up and I hated looking at myself. At Queen's house, there were pictures of me actually smiling. I looked like someone cared about me. I was healthy and all of my needs were met. I had no complaints.

Chapter 9

I was entering middle school and I felt my body changing. I started to like the opposite sex a little more. I was trying my best to figure out where i belonged. I didnt quite feel secure enough to express all my personal issues or my life at school. It was different cliques in my school. I was always with the different crews i was what you called a set hopper. I liked everyone. I just wanted friends. I didn't have much knowledge about the opposite sex, so I would do things i would see the fast girls do . Alot of my friends already had an idea of who they were. I couldn't believe kids this young even had similar problems. Their problems weren't like mine though. They didn't have family issues. They had small issues like who broke up with who or can i cheat off your homework. I made some great friends. Not knowing myself made me different people. I still couldtn trust like i wanted to or build healthy relationships. I was always cautious because anything could change. Peer pressure was at an all time high as well. I was still well behaved, but i liked to test the waters from time to time. Queen let me hang out with my friends. She even let me travel with one of my close friends that I made in middle school. She let me explore more of myself and figure out who I was. I respected her for that. I still had underlying issues inside, but being there made me forget what I left behind. I wanted to feel better inside and fix what was wrong. No one seemed to understand my pain, so i hid the part of me always. I was more involved in church at the time so school activities didn't matter. Even though I couldn't quite grasp what the pastor was saying I knew I wanted to attend church because silly boy was there. Some time passed and I started to visit my aunt. She seemed very happy and seeing her made me miss her. Whatever happened in the past was never brought up. I felt like she was avoiding being asked the important questions I was curious about. I wanted to know everything she had going on in her present life. She was more concerned of who I grew up to be. We did things a growing teen would be interested in. She taught me how to wear eyeliner and she taught me how to put a tampon in. The first try was tragic but she walked me through it. She got me my first pair of zero jeans. Those jeans meant your hips were spreading. They became my favorite jeans until my bottom grew bigger. I didn't want to get rid of them because I held onto things that my family gave me. My aunt and I became sisters and I didn't want that feeling to go away. I called her all the time just to hear her voice. She became someone i knew would help me through all the confusion in my head. I was very happy to see her life was her own again. I would brag about her as we got closer. She became the cool aunt that made anything possible. I shared my feelings for boys with her. We talked about school. I was sure to keep it at the level of an aunt and niece relationship. She also let me express myself the way i wanted. When I got my menstrual cycle balancing my emotions became so hard. My body was going through changes and my facial expressions showed it. I was sure to keep every area on me clean because I didn't want to get teased again. When someone picked on me about a flaw I made it a priority to fix it so they wouldn't have anything to talk about. At Queen's, I finally got what I was yearning for. I had a family there, but I was still missing something. I became a little more confidentl. I stared in the mirror more even though I hated how I looked. I started to apply tissue to my shirt to feel more like a woman. I would stuff tissue in my shirt because I was so flat-chested like a little boy. As I continued to grow,I grew to have huge breasts the size of watermelons. It was like everything I wished for I eventually got but . Those things brought negative attention. I wore three bras sometimes to hide them. The things I prayed for I got and when i got them i had more problems. Queen didn't have any foster kids in her home but my sister and i, That changed and Queen got a new foster child. I didn't know what to think of her, but I was in the family now and no one was going to take my place. I felt very entitled. As long as she stayed out my way we wouldn't have any issues. When I met the new girl, She reminded me of myself . She was falling apart from not being home with her family. At first, I wanted to dislike her because she cried too much but disliking her wouldn't help me in any way. She was hurt and I didn't want to hurt her even more. I could relate to her in many ways due to her situation, but i wanted to grow from my hurt. I tried my best to help her look at her situation in a different light. We became close once I heard her story. She eventually got used to how things worked around the house. She was in high school and I was in my last year of middle school. I told her everything about my life. We became really close. Her story was similar,she expressed herself freely and wasn't afraid to cry out loud. I applaud her for that, but I just couldn't let anyone see how ugly I looked crying. We became a dynamic duo. I grew more and more in church. I joined that step team and even started to attend church events with the other members' children. I still had a huge crush on a silly boy which everyone knew. Queen would ask me about it all the time but I would deny it. I didnt think my feelings even mattered. I was happy at queens. I had a family, but they weren't my own . I felt so bad adopting another one. I didn't think this was normal at all. We made memories together and my life was going in the right direction. I had little insecurities that made me shy. Queen nephew picked on me about my acne. He would call me pizza face. Puberty hit me hard. I ignored him at times, but I started to feel I was really ugly. I also had this crooked lip. When i talk my lip would go to the side. I had no control over it. Sometimes I was afraid to talk in front of people. He was like this popular kid that everyone loved at school and home.

I believed what he said was true. I felt at home,I felt loved, I didn't feel judged but he was the only one that brought attention to my flaws all the time. I tried my best to laugh it off and not let him see that his words were tearing me apart. He wasn't with his family either so i felt he had no room to put me down.

My church crush liked me so his opinion didn't matter. I started to grow stronger feelings for this silly boy at church.We rarely talked.We just stared at one another or I would say hello and run away. I wrote Queen a letter asking her if I was allowed to talk to him on the house phone and slid it under her door. She was huge on honesty. I couldn't hide these feelings . I finally had the courage to ask. I was so nervous and didn't know where the courage came from. I ran into my room and waited for her to address my request. She said yes! I just knew she would tell me no but she didn't.The terms we agreed on of course had regulations. He was allowed to call before nine oclock. I hogged the phone at times.We had one phone line in the house.When our time exceeded the time we were supposed to get off the phone queen would embarrass me the other phone. It was so embarrassing but funny at the same time. I was too young to know what a boyfriend was, but these were normal feelings teens developed. I felt good inside. Someone actually liked me for me.We talked on the phone for hours. I sometimes snuck on the phone when I wasn't supposed to. He was everything I could imagine, nice but rebellious. His family attended the church as well . If i didn't see them then he wasn't at church. Like any other curious teen, we had to have our first kiss. It was in the stairwell of the church. I knew for sure I was going to burn in hell.The good times didn't last long before drama followed us.Another girl claimed to like him and deal with him as well. He thought he was a player, but he didn't know i had two sides to me. I couldn't have this girl ruining what I worked so hard to get.What was mine belonged to me.At times I thought we were sharing him because she was trying to compromise with me. I tried my hardest to ignore her, but she was always there. He had to choose and I prayed it would be me. I couldn't believe someone

I thought was for me had options. I thought I was being played. So I started to play as well. I lost interest in him over time because he didn't know what he wanted and he began to change his ways. I didn't like change so I tried to put him behind me. I saw him all the time which made it awkward. His friends and I were still friends, but of course their loyalty lies with him. I felt they were whispering every time I walked past. After him I wanted that feeling again, but this time from an older guy. I didn't like the immature boys anymore. I felt my brain developed faster than others by force. I didn't look at him in the same way after the drama. Time passed by and things were going well. I swept the old news under the rug with the other crap I had buried. I wanted to explore the world. I wanted to see what Queen was protecting me from. Even if Queen had strict rules I was eager to see what the world had to offer me. I tried my best to respect her rules, but my curiosity was starving . My body was still growing and the urges grew overnight. I looked at the moon every night just wondering what would make me happy and whole. Memories with my family faded. I couldn't even remember them anymore. Rage grew in me and I couldn't show it or control it. One night a few of us were watching a movie and a sexual scene came on. I made a joke that I was having these tingly feelings inside. I was joking around and blurted it out,but my sister ran upstairs and snitched on me. I thought it was something wrong with me, but I couldn't even enjoy it in peace because she snitched. Queen didn't overreact, but she was quick to schedule a doctor's appointment for birth control. The doctor explained why I was having those feelings, I was so relieved that they were normal hormonal changes. Queen told me it was to regulate my menstrual, but I think the Queen was taking precautions. The pill made me so sick I would forget to take them on purpose. I wasn't sexual involved with anyone. The pills made me so sick so I tossed them. My new best friend at Queen's house loved high school and I wanted to know everything about it. She told me how she became friends with this hot freshman. I liked everything I was hearing so I told her to hook us up. I had never even seen this guy a day in my life. For all, he knew I could have been missing an ear. I was desperate.

Surely after she told him he was interested. We wrote one another letters and sent them through her. I shared everything with Queen's oldest daughter because I trusted her. She was like the popular rebel child. She didn't judge me at all. Our bond was so dope she was the best big sister I could ask for. I wrote my high school crush so much that he wanted to see me. I didn't know how I was going to pull that off. One day my best friend came home from school and he was right behind her. I could have died that day. She wasn't thinking straight that day. Queen would have drowned us both in holy oil. He didn't come anywhere near the house, but I believe he wanted to see who he was writing. We exchanged numbers. I told him never call me, I would call him. For all Queen knew I was still dating a silly boy at church. I started to become more independent and wanted more freedom which I knew she wasn't going to give me. So I took it. I was so eager to see highschool crush. we were dating for some time now. I was feeling myself. One afternoon Queen was going out of town and big sister was in charge. I snuck him and a friend over from the back door. My heart was racing through my chest. Queen rarely came in the basement so I knew it was the perfect plan. I got too ahead of myself because Queen must have forgotten something and came back home. I hurried to put everything back in place. I was too late and she knew I was up to something. From that day I knew she wasn't for my shenanigans. I had to come up with a better plan to see the man of my dreams. I walked home from school every day and would get home before any of the other kids. I couldn't wait until my best friend got home to see what messages my boyfriend sent my way. He had so many questions about why I couldn't come out of the house or have company. I brushed it off and told him I would see him soon. Soon came too soon. I began to walk home with kids that lived near him. That would be my excuse to see him . I didn't know what I was getting myself into I just knew I had it all under control. I really didn't but I knew how to be quick on my feet. We arranged that I would come to see him at his house. That day came and I wanted to change my mind. I wasn't a coward so I went. I was shaking so bad I just knew he was going to try something. He didn't and i was relieved. He was well mannered. I met his dad. His dad was asking questions as if we were getting married. I was allowed in his room. We just had to keep the room door open. This was better than B's house, so I enjoyed it. I think he was nervous as well because he was talking to his dad while I sat on his bed. As I was sitting, I scoped his room out. His wallet was on the dresser so I opened it and looked at his identification. I heard him coming so I hurried to sit back down. We talked for a while. Both of us were cheesing from ear to ear. I kept checking the time because I had to at least beat Queen home. His eyes made it very clear that he wasn't new to this and my eyes made it very clear that I wasn't ready. I ended the visit quickly. He walked me to the end of the block to make sure I got across the busy street safely. I just knew I was in love because I didn't even want to run normally. The cars could hit me and I'd still think of him. I was a grade behind. I belong in the 9th grade with everyone else but that's another secret I was afraid to tell anyone. Time went by and things were perfect for me. We were months into our relationship and I think I was ready to give myself to him. Despite what I learned in church about saving myself until mar- riage, I knew this feeling was what they were referring to. I felt i was in love. Queen had no clue I felt this way about him. She didn't even know about him. I would told her little things, but my sister knew all the lat- est. Queen and i didnt talk about boys. In that area I made my own decisions. At a point in time, I think parents just let their children's curiosity stage happen. Queen had many conversations indirectly about things we needed to be aware of, but she never directly told us real life examples. Kevin and i were dating for some time now and I finally wanted it to be official. We both talked about my first time being spe- cial, but he wasn't a virgin which bothered me. I didn't make a big deal. At church they always said "No sex before marriage". I wanted to fol- low that way of life. .The marriage couples at church seemed so happy and free. My feelings still werent taken inconsideration, so i did things my way. I walked to his house with confidence, but the walk seemed longer because I knew I was making a bad choice. I talked to myself the whole time. I arrived and we talked once more about it. I had to make sure this was a forever thing before anything. I agreed to give it to him. Earlier that day Queen shared some terrible news that broke me. I was more eager to do it out of anger than anything. He was straight forward with it. I was trying to remember what I saw in the movie just so it would look as if i knew what i was doing. He took complete control. We laid down, we exchanged kisses,he looked in my eyes and started touching my body. He told me to remove my clothes and relax. He took his time. I was so scared. As he entered my body I felt like my innocence left my body. . It didn't hurt as much,but I had a bad feeling that giving him this power was a bad idea. After I broke my hymen everything changed. I was so excited to tell my big sister this had happened to me, but the moment wasn't worth what I thought I was missing. Where was the horse and carriage? There was no magic to it at all. Little after I gave him my soul he gave me his ass to kiss. He became so nonchalant to my feelings that I just knew I had learned my third life lesson. Obey your parents! Our relationship had become so emotionally toxic that some days I wanted to cut my wrist. I fell back into a bubble because I felt I was giving people too much of me. At home, things were still going great until Queen told us that it was official that we were moving to another part of town. I was so mad that we had to leave. I was just getting used to life here and i didnt want to leave. I didn't want to move so I came up with a plan to run away. One night my best friend and I stayed out and didn't come back. We didn't have a plan nor did we know where to go. I knew we could crash at Kevin's house. When we arrived at his house his dad thought our reasoning was silly and talked us into returning home. We stayed at his house as long as we could until night came then we had to leave. We went to the playground by my school and slept in an opening where no one would see us. That was the most uncomfortable sleep ever. I sat and thought for a very long time. I noticed my anger was creeping out even more. Only this time it was actions behind it. I wasn't using my brain at all. The next day we decided to return home. Queen had a talk with us and boy was I scared. My best friend ended up leaving me a few months later. She was the only one I could talk to and I got her into this mess. I was

SOME PLACE TO GROW

bringing others into my troubles. Weeks went by and things kinda went back to normal. I could feel how disappointed queen was at me. Graduation was coming and things were about to change drastically. She knew I wouldn't make it in the local high school. She made comments like "they will eat you alive". She was so dramatic, but even she knew what was best for me and I trusted her before anything. Her mindset was very Godly but living in the real world I felt she was supposed to teach me basic rules to survive. Looking back now, having that Godly mindset is what protected us from the world.

I was okay with the decision to move. I didn't have a choice, but once again change was very terrifying for me. My relationship was saveable,but he showed me what we had could be replaced. I went over to end things with him. I explained that I was moving and we could try the long-distance thing. He acted as if it wouldn't work. I started to think it was in men's nature to go after this one thing that only women possessed. I didn't need him to walk me to the end of the street like he always did because I was never coming down that street again. I walked out of the door and started to walk as fast as I could. Tears began to fall down my face. I got halfway to the end of the street and I heard my name being called. I kept walking because I didn't want to look back. His voice got closer and closer to me. I turned around and it was him running to me. He picked me up and wiped my face and told me he would be here for me no matter what. It was such a relief for me. I believed him once again, but that didn't last. He became so inconsistent in the last week of our move. I didn't hold on,I let him go. The hurt of him not trying stuck with me. I didn't speak to him for days then weeks. Moving day came. For what I knew I was getting just what I deserved. I developed a deep hatred towards men which made me want revenge.

Chapter 10

We moved further this time. The house was built from the ground up. We Road through the neighborhood and all I saw were Caucasian people. My middle school was diverse, but I never saw so many Caucasians in my life. I wasn't sure why Queen chose this area. I needed a fresh slate. She knew what was best so I shut my mouth. At this point it felt like i was running away from my problems. As we drove she showed me the local high school I would be attending. It was months before I would officially start. I had no choice but to prepare for the life of high school. My moods started to change tremendously. I didn't want anyone to think I was crazy. I tried my best to keep my attitude together. It only came out when I didn't get my way. I didn't like anyone telling me no. Pops had to talk to me more and more, which was weird because he rarely spoke. He just gave the eye and we knew he was upset. I had a hard time accepting no because I felt so much was taken away, and I was entitled to everything. I had it made here but I just didn't appreciate it.

Our new home was beautiful . I have never seen anything like it. Who knew a city orphan would live in a mansion. We had our own garage that could fit two cars in it. I saw this on mtv one time. Actually living in a mansion was breathtaking . The house had 4 rooms upstairs with a balcony that connected each side, if you looked over the balcony the living room was on one side. The kitchen was huge and the basement was big as a movie theater. Not much play area in the backyard, but we were getting older so we didn't have time for play. As we settled in our new home our routine was pretty much the same. We didn't have many chores anymore because we were always busy. I became exhausted with everything. I had to sneak naps in. Prayer, step practice, and church events all summer. That summer i tried my best to get back right with God . It was like I was forcing it because I knew i was making mistakes. My thoughts didn't run as fast as they used to but I still wanted that feeling that I was enough. I wanted to feel like i was worth something. I wanted to be enough for someone to love. At prayer on tuesday, I closed my eyes and fell into deep thought. I created so many scenarios in my head that lead to the lord coming to my rescue every time. We prayed for about thirty minutes. My knees were aching by the time we were finished. I had so much to talk to God about. I had pretty great relationships in church that kept me grounded. I had two mentors that helped me sperate what was the devil's work and what was God's work. I listened but I was so sure I knew it all. My sister and I attended a 4 weeks seminar at church called I HAVE STANDARDS. Alot of the mentors at my church lead the class, so I was comfortable attending. They taught us about our worth, what to accept in life, and how God should be the answer to everything. I believed they were truthful about the things they taught us. I wanted to actually feel it and apply it to my life on my own. I couldn't because i was so focused on other things in life. I failed the purity class. I wanted to a second chance at making things right with myself. I didn't hear much from my biological mother as much as i got older. That hurt me that i had to force a mother and daughter relationship with a stranger. I wanted to talk to my mother and tell her all the great things i've experienced since she's been gone. She was hard to reach and my my feelings for her turned into stone. I still had a consistent relationship with my aunt, She moved a few blocks from our church. Some days I would walk to her house just to check on her. Eventually queen let me stay the weekend. I grew to not miss my parents even more. Seeing my aunt created hope and possibility of seeing my parents again. I randomly seen my siblings on different occasions but they weren't the same. You could tell their experience after being separated from the family had changed them for the worse It was too late to cover them with my security blanket. My brothers and i didnt have that connection anymore. That feeling of togetherness was gone. As I got older queen encouraged me to reconnect with my biological family more. She was very family oriented so i understand why she wanted that for me. I wasn't ready though. Seeing my family just made me weaker. I was happy at queens and my lifestyle did not compare to my old life growing up. My walk had an appealing posture, my talk was proper, and I frowned upon going back to my old life. I felt like I adapted to my environment to survive. I didn't want to just exist i wanted to live. I felt I gravitated towards what would get me noticed. I did things that would get me popularity. I was called "bougie" or a white girl. I was fine with being called that as long as no one called me poor or made fun of my past. Sometimes I was happy being called those names because Caucasians seemed so free and happy and I wanted my life to be just like that.

I was free to be who I was in my teenage years. Queen didn't pressure me about going to church as long as we had one foot in the door. I still attended but life and responsibilities started to kick in. We all had a family car that was passed down to each of us. The car was a gift from pop's mother. I was next in line and very excited to drive because all the kids in high school had cars. Queen and I started practicing. Pop helped me as well. I was so determined to pass the test. I failed the written part the first time but then I went back and took it again and passed. I walked out head held high and proud of myself. We were still settling in the new home. High School was approaching and I knew some of my neighbors attended that school so I became friends with them. Our bus stop was almost a mile from the house. I hated that because in the winter time I would freeze to death walking. I didn't know what to expect in high school. All I knew was the first fresh start and I was in a new place where no one knew me. The first day came and the school was flooded with Caucasian people. I choose to say Caucasians because I respect everyone's race but there were maybe twenty african American students. In middle school, it seemed as if there were more African Americans because we stuck together as a group, but here I couldn't find a single black person. I could feel my anxiety flaring up. I was in my head alot at this school. I talked to myself more than ever. I wanted to fit in and feel accepted but i was so afraid . I never been so afraid in my life. Some of my teachers and staff were very nice but the other half was rude and treated my kind like they knew we would fail. I had this! It wasn't a obstacle i couldn't get through. I knew what I had to do. I had to stay quiet until I got a feel of how things operate at this school. I saw my neighbors at school so that made me feel a little comfortable. They were new as well but they had a better chance at blending in than me. I was just curious to know what people thought of me and how they saw me. I wasn't sure if what I felt inside was enough. I seeked others' validation. I went to my classes and tried my best. I tried to stay on top of my grades but i was worried about fitting in. My inner child came out in some of my classes purposely. I was tired of always being so serious. Even though I was quiet, I had a fire in me that was waiting to explode. Weeks went by, I wanted to join different activities and groups. I started staying after for football games and clubs they offered. I made a couple of friends during the first few weeks but nothing major. At this point in my life relationships were not so important to me. My humility for others was turned off. I was very selfish and only cared about making me happy whatever it took. I wasnt so much into my appearance like the other kids were. I was a plain jane and I liked it. I kept my appearance up but material things don't faze me at all. I was fresh meat at ths school. I didn't want to step on anyone's toes, but at the same time i wanted trouble. I met a football player that was in the eleventh. He was super charming and very tall. We exchanged numbers and became friends. Things were good at first but I saw right through him. He wasn't honest with me about things. I got the wrath of his past. His ex-girlfriend didn't like me one

CHAPTER 10

bit. I was the topic of conversation in a few cliques. That didn't last because he couldn't be honest with me. I'm glad I didn't give him any of my goods. After Kevin, I closed the shop down. We remained friends because he was charming. He tried to play me and it didn't work. Months in and I made more and more friends. I joined clubs and helped out a lot of my teachers. Academically I was very distracted. I attended class but mind was on everything else. School was a place for me to find myself when i wasn't home. I know it sounds crazy, but I wasn't a troubled teen so I wanted to act up a little just to see the attention I would receive. At home, things were pretty calm. I didn't have time to get in trouble at home because I was too tired from being in school doing absolutely nothing. I learned the different cliques and I wanted to know at least one or two people from their group. I Had chinese friends,asian,indian,and hispanic friends. I liked being different and my different friends accepted me. My black friends normalized copying one another for popularity. I gravitated towards that too because they made it look fun. We had a step team that I joined and guess what, the football player's ex was in charge. That didn't stop me. I still joined. A lot of my confidence came from my peers. They gave me a feeling of importance. I walked around that school like I knew I was the sugar honey iced tea. Deep inside it took everything in me not to show any-one my weakness. My life was great, but I had an identity crisis. I started to feel like who I was becoming wasn't me. It was nice at first. I was happy. I started to step out of my box, but then I realized i was this poor girl from the city that can't even tell my truth. I was struggling inside. I had to keep pushing which was hard for me. I couldn't trust people or gain genuine relationships because I didn't know how. I was still damaged by my past. I reminded myself every day because I didn't want to forget. I was pretty comfortable at my school even though I was a grade behind . Queen took it upon herself to see if it was pos-sible that I took more credits to graduate with my class. She challenged me in all areas of my life. I just couldn't see the bigger picture. She pushed me to my full potential. I was placed in my right grade for the next school year. I had to attend summer school to take a course I couldn't take during the school year. It was awkward because many questions were asked. I was so afraid to tell the truth so most of the time I hid behind lies. I used to say I resent her for what she didn't teach me about the world, but she set me up for my future and I'm forever grateful for her. Of course, I had to take summer school for credit but I was happy that I was graduating on time. In highschool i pretty much struggled with my identity,but I grew to learn new things about the world around me. I chose to be a good person despite cultural differences. I built a few solid relationships that meant the world to me while i was in school. I made one best friend whom I still talk to till this day. We were inseparable in highschool. You would have thought we came out of the same womb. We did everything together. She had the face of a goddess and the purest heart. She was very popular. We instantly clicked. We told one another everything . Well almost everything. She didn't know my truth. I figured she had an idea of it, but she didn't want to ask. It was many times I wanted to tell her but I didn't want her to look at me any other way or judge me. I was good at occupying my time at school. I became the basketball manager for the girl's basketball team. I didn't choose the boys team because i didn't want anyone calling me a groupie. I took my job seriously. I was a black manager on a all white team. I thought i was comfortable,but at times i wouldn't fully do the job. The team always invited me out to dinner and i would respectfully decline. I wasn't ready to tackle on racial problems in school being the minority. It was bad enough i felt like was surrounded by racist staff and teachers. I found many reasons to stay after school. I had to find rides home because queen was always at church. It was either go to church or stay after and hang out with friends. A ride home was easy to find because I didn't want to attend church even though I needed it. I wasn't the type to come off so strong when it came to meeting guys but at one of the basketball games,I saw this guy from the other team. I had my eyes on him the entire game. My best friend introduced us . He was such a gentleman so I knew he would get introduced to the family. He was kind, cute, dark, and played ball. I knew I had to watch out for those type. He seemed different. His spirit was warm. Queen allowed me to talk to boys and date the old fashion way. She didn't want me to spend so much time with him even though I wanted to see him every day. I couldn't believe that the feeling I wanted again was right in my face. We dated for a while. Things got pretty serious but no official title. That relationship ended fast as well. We were just in two different places in life. We were good friends years after . After that relationship I didn't want anything serious because nothing ever lasted with me it seemed. I had multiple guy friends texting my phone. I felt now I should have really taken the time to heal me and get my mind together. but I was too far gone to see it that way. If men wanted to play games,I wanted to play them too. I got so wrapped up in this boy crazy world. I got distracted and Queen could sense it. She thought it was a great idea that I start applying for jobs. I applied for clothing stores in the mall and a retirement home. I dreaded applying for fast food jobs because I knew it would be hard dealing with the ignorant public. Some of my friends had jobs and drove. I wanted the same thing. I was next in line for the family car. Some times i was able to drive to school. I couldn't believe i was accomplishing yet another goal. I didn't want to walk anymore and would tell my friends to pick me up for school. I had to show the queen I was trustworthy. Most times I acted as if I didn't have a care in the world. I received good news that I got the job at the retirement home. Queen was the only one that kept me in line and focus. I didn't want to let her down in any way. The thought of leaving the nest was the day i fall flat to my face. I was excited to start work and have my own money. Queen would pretend she was my bank to help me save. Every check i received queen helped me save a percentage of it. I wasn't sure I would like the experience of working with old folks, but it was the best experience in my life. I met some rich folks, I learned proper etiquette skills, and I met some great friends from different schools. On top of that, they gave us a scholarship for college. Some days I had to walk home from work because the queen schedule clashed with mine. I hated the walk,I cried sometimes while walking home. I had to figure out another way. After school I would get on a friend's bus to make sure I would be on time for work. Some days i didn't see my family because when I got in from work it was shower and sleep. I liked staying busy and I liked my own money, but the responsibility was becoming a lot. I eventually earned enough money to get my own cell phone and pay my own bills. Nothing else mattered at that point. I was in my own world. Some days I would skip dinner just to be on the phone all night. I ran up the bill one summer and had to pay almost five hundred dollars back. I had that much to discuss with my friends. We had free minutes after nine so everyone had to call me around bedtime. Text messaging was free though. My schedule was so out of whack and I became overwhelmed. I wasn't a little girl anymore and I felt it. I started to become sassier and sassier because I didn't like growing up. Queen and I started to disagree on a lot of things, but it was her house so I had to abide by her rules until I went to college. She didn't let us get tattoos or piercings until we were eighteen. When that time came to get tattoos I rushed and got the randomest tattoos. I regret every tattoo I ever got looking back. As kids, we don't really see the significance of why our parents tell us no, but I wish I would have listened. A lot of times I was the bolder in my way. I wanted to learn better ways to problem-solve, better life skills, better social skills and even better ways of understanding how my emotions work.

School was still going well for me. I started to focus more and really take life seriously. My academics, work and graduating was what I focused on. A lot of friends changed on me. I made enemies because I was too nice. I didn't have a voice to say what I really wanted to say so I let pointless relationships go. I wasn't a confrontational personal at all. Some days I adapted to my so-called friends around me. I didn't know who I was which made it a lot worse. I felt myself choosing them over myself and i didnt like it at all. My school was very big on school spirit. We didn't have junior prom which I will never understand why. I wanted to go to prom because most of my friends were asked to the seniors proms. I attended a church member's son's prom. We were good friends at the time. He spoke little words to me. He was very sweet. I was into bad boys so i looked past him. I don't know why i was attracted to the wrong ones. I knew i needed serious help because i was attracted to the most toxic situations when it came to boys. That was one area i struggled with. He had a themed prom, I was plain jane once again. I wasn't into fashion so I didn't know what was in and what wasn't. Queen and I searched for a dress that matched his suit. I hated my hair, nothing went right that night. I wasn't very secure with myself. When I felt that way I became very quiet. When we arrived at the prom I felt everyone making fun of me. I didn't want to make his prom a nightmare so I sat to the side and let him enjoy himself. I really wanted to run again. I wanted this night to be over. I wish I could tell him I'm sorry for humiliating him. My senior prom came and I went with the most handsome guy in the school. I was more excited to see my friends because this was our last year together. I liked my school because we had homecoming and different activities I looked forward to. Looking back maybe Queen thought I would pick up on bad habits at that zone school and she was right.

I was proud to say I graduated from my high school because it taught me a lot about myself. Graduation came and we said our goodbyes and cried our eyes out. I wasn't ready for real life but I had no choice. It was time to leave the nest. Queen gave me a graduation party, I felt so loved. I was very nervous inside. None of my biological family was there, but my church family and friends were all I needed. I was going to be alone again and that terrified me. I wasn't ready to leave my life. I was happy at Queen's. I had never been so happy in my life. I had no desire of reuniting with my parents, but I wish she prepared me for what might come if I ever did. Even though I had great people around me, inside I was always thinking when will they leave? Was I good enough to be in these people's lives for them to stay? I felt so lost because I wanted to heal those unknown feelings that were building up. I didn't have time to figure out any solution because time did not stop for me so I couldn't stop for my problems.

I was ahead of my game in a lot of ways and in alot of areas i ways i was behind. Queen set me up to win. i owed it to her. I had to really understand and realize that I wouldn't be here if it wasn't for God or Queen's family. They created an ideal women. I had someone else in me. Some days the rage inside of me was seeping out. I fought hard to keep it hidden. I had everything I could imagine, but I couldn't understand why my own parents couldn't see how important I was. Why did it take someone else's family to show me how valuable I was?

I always wanted to share how I felt with Queen, but I didn't want her to think that I was unappreciative of her and all of her hard work. I swept how I felt under the rug, but I started to get in the habit of finding things to fill that void. I felt I was missing something. Instead of expressing my feelings, I found things to feed those negative thoughts. I had sexual intercourse when I didn't really want to. The attention and touch made me feeling important. The fact that someone wanted to touch me and be close to me made me feel secure. I was always told no sex before marriage. I didnt know the importance of waiting for that intimate connection between a husband and wife. I didnt have the patience to wait to understand it either. Making decision for myself felt good, but deep down i knew these choices werent good for my soul. Summer break was officially here and I had some time to play. I hung out with friends, worked and enjoyed the extra hours i didn't have at school. Queen was still running a tight home. She didn't yell as much because we were adults and knew better. Before school ended i researched some colleges. I had options but i didn't want to go to far from home. College was slowly approaching and I had half the summer to enjoy before college orientation started. I was meeting new guys and rushing the process of getting to know them. I started to get into new troubles just because. I didn't have a reason behind it. I wanted to actually feel what it was like to be free. I developed a terrible habit of letting people in me if they told me they liked me. I was vulnerable to a certain extent as well as desperate for love. I honestly didn't know why those feelings erupted the way they did but despite my actions, I kept my behavior hidden. I noticed as I continued to make those harsh choices my value went down. I didn't care who was affected by my actions until I lost some real friendships and relationships. I didn't quite understand the damage of betrayal so I kept it going to make myself feel whole. My bad habits became an addiction. I was preparing for the biggest opportunity of my life. I would be the second in my family to complete college if I would have finished. I didn't think I would find love again and I didn't have it within me so I didn't have anything to look forward to. I disrespected myself in many ways and I turned into a monster and I needed that help to figure out why.

Chapter 11

I couldn't wait to explain this chapter of my life. It's the most confusing thing ever. I fell in love with the kindest man. he was so selfless. I've been through some men and I went against my type for once. I fell for his spirit. He brightens every dark place in my body. My biological family knew his family. I wanted to know him personally for myself, I didn't care how my family knew him. All I cared about was that he wasn't blood related. We lived in two totally different worlds. I was very happy that he didn't really know anything about my past or what I was capable of. I was just happy to have a clean slate with someone. He was a challenge, he was mysterious and he kept me on my toes. It's funny how everything comes into play because I saw him at the movie theater often when I hung out with my friends. The mall and movies is where all the inner city kids came to hang out. Seeing his face often made me curious about who he was. I thought it was fate. One night I went joy riding around with my older sister. We wanted to attend the Bow Wow concert but the queen wasn't having that so we drove to the let out. I saw him on the corner with the same friend he was always at the movies with. I yelled his name and he looked my way. He probably was freaked out by my raspy voice. I just knew he would be my man. I got his number from a cousin of mine. I was so nervous to actually reach out to him. He never actually saw me,i felt like a stalker.

I was so nervous at first. My impulse said go for it or else you'll miss the opportunity. We started texting and getting to know one another. The connection was instantly there. This was the connection I needed. I was so used to dealing with guys sexualy because of my pain. With him i didn't think that way. I was meeting him for the first time. We met up at my Aunt's house to talk which turned into a routine thing. We sat on the curb and talked all night. I wanted to know everything about him. He was so nice. I wanted to know if he had another side to him. I felt it was a story deep within him. I was hesitant to tell him all about me, but in the back of my mind if I wanted him to be the one. I would have to be honest with him and I was afraid. He was respectful, calm, and he was different from the way I would normally date. It felt like he was trying to find himself as well. I wanted us to do it together. I had two months to make him mine before I went to college so I was determined. We spent a lot of time together from that day on. We started spending more time at his house. I had more freedom there. His mother didn't ask many questions. We made out non stop until our lips turned blue. I was surprised I didn't contract mono. That's what most of the Caucasian girls complained about in high school. I took my time with him because he was special. He was emotionally there for me as well. Queen went out of town again, only this time I didn't have to really sneak. I felt i had more self control with him. I made plans for him to come to my house. My older sister was in charge. She was the fun one that let us do anything. Him and his friend were in disbelief when they saw how I lived. They thought my parents were rich. It was always a question in my head, if he knew they were not my real parents. He never made me feel any less if he did know my secret. I couldn't tell how he really felt about me because he wasn't a man of many words he was more so an action man. Everything seemed right with him so I went with the flow. I wasn't sure if I really liked him either at times. He had everything figured out. I didn't want to disturb his life with all of my issues. I tried to push him away but he solved every problem i had. When my sister told me he had come to visit, I was actually on the phone with another guy. Stupid move I know. I ended that conversation fast and got myself together to see him.

This new guy kept me on my toes, and I wasn't messing it up. I wanted the bad habits to die off. He helped me cope most of the time. I was so attracted to his rich dark skin. He had long locks, He was skinny, not real short. He was just the right height. I was attracted to lighter skinned boys. They were what you called pretty boys. I went to the dark side after kevin. I needed to step out of my comfort zone. We started to spend so much time together and I fell fast because of his presence. He showed me he wanted me to be in his life. We talked for hours every night. Sometimes we sat in the car and just exchanged our thoughts. He was such a charming man. He was so generous as well. He actaully lifted my strong hatred for men. He put me before himself. He attended church with me a few times so I knew he was the one. We moved very fast but chemistry wouldn't let us slow down. Summer time was winding down and I had almost one week left until college orientation started. The orientation was a week long. I thought I would die without him. After the orientation it was the start of a new life and I didnt think I was ready. I wanted a degree for myself and my family. My strong feelings had to be put on hold for a week. That week of orientation was the longest. He was on my mind the entire time. I didn't have a cell phone to contact him because we had to turn them in. I chose a historically black college. This was a very new experience for me. I wanted the full experience.

During orientation I met new friends, it was a different environment for me. The campus was so afrocentric, I knew i had a lot to learn about my own culture that i didn't know. I couldn't wait to get home to him. I think Queen was getting the picture that I really liked him. He became my universe. She gave me a going away party which was emotional. I thought my world was ending. He attended the party but I know he felt out of place. He really didn't know the family that raised me. My lifestyle there probably made him feel out of place. I had his back in every way though. I was falling in love and starting a new chapter at the same time. We talked that entire night before i departed. I hugged him about a hundred times, and kissed a thousand times. I felt like I was in a movie. My foot would literally pop up everytime we kissed. I was sure he put a spell on me. I appreciated how he showed me how a woman is supposed to be treated. Goodbyes wasn't that bad for me. I played usher Burn that entire night and cried my eyes out. College move-in day came and I didnt know what to expect. I was going to a historically black college and I didn't know what my life was going to be like there but i was ready. I was feeling myself. I wanted a new hairstyle. I had a talk with myself to boost my confidence for this big change. I got my first weave in my hair. Extensions were the thing at the time. I still had the same one way of calling a cricket phone that I hated. No one could get through if I was on the phone. Years back when I was transitioning to high school. I remember the Queen saying she didn't want me to attend the local high school because they would eat me alive. I didn't know what she meant by that, but once I went to college I figured it out. There were black sexy men everywhere. The guys were drooling over me. I was in a relationship though. I was a freshman and I was fresh meat to half the campus. I've always attended a school where it was predominantly Caucasian kids. This experience because I had lost touch with my culture. I never learned about African or African American history in high school. I pulled up to this huge tower, unloading my storage and settling in my room. I still had some emotional concerns and personal issues. Those feelings were not going to ruin anything for me. I didn't want anyone to think I was crazy once again. Was I crazy?

I made a few friends from the orientation so I instantly was in search of them. I unpacked my stuff and took a deep breath. My mom and dad said their goodbyes and left. This was my first time being independent. I was used to being alone emotionally. I wasn't working at the time. The state gave me a stipend every month for things I needed. I appreciated it because I didn't have to call home for anything. After I unpacked and called my boyfriend instantly. We used Skype all the time. I had to balance trying to be social, getting my school work done, and having a boyfriend. It was a lot, but I felt I could do all three. When I started my classes I couldn't talk to him, and he understood it. A few months went by and we decided it was time for me to come home on weekends. He drove forty five minutes away just to pick me up. I wanted a degree but I was more focused on filling these emotional voids. I wanted love so badly that my future had to wait. I didn't tell my parents I was home because I was engaging in ungodly behaviors. I stayed at my sister's house or either his mother's house. This relationship was different. I wanted this forever. I was balancing my grades and our relationship. One of them wasn't going to get my full attention. I spent so much time with him. Final grades came out and I was very satisfied with them. I started to hang out more with my friends and spend less time on the phone with him. Things started to become weird to me. He wouldn't answer or I couldn't get a hold of him. In my mind he was cheating but I didn't care because every guy wanted me. The thought was still in the back of my head. I didn't need the attention I was getting at school so I stayed inside my dorm most of the time. I started to feel he couldn't handle the distance. I just needed his word and that he gave me so I trusted him. One day we had a long talk and he told me he took a female to the movies and he kissed her. I could have killed him and buried him myself with no help. He wasn't that big in weight so i knew i could get the job done. I ignored his calls for days because I thought I finally trusted and loved someone. All my hard work was for nothing I felt like. The last person that told me they loved me left me and I was sure to leave him. I couldn't leave him though,he broke down walls i built since i was a young girl. I was in love. I was also a fighter. He was young and had a lot going for himself so I know a lot of females wanted him. I was scared of myself because deep down inside I didn't care about his actions. I was used to being let down. As much as I said I didn't care, it made me want revenge. This time I wanted my actions to show how I was really feeling. This situation really retraumatized me. I started to flirt with guys and engage in illegal activities. I even tried smoking marijuana for the first time with my girls. I wanted new trouble because that's what I turned to when I was hurting. I couldn't hide it. Why couldn't I use what I was going through emotionally as motivation to get me where I needed to be logically. I started to party more and attend every frat party. He noticed that I was acting differently and I wanted him to. One Friday he came to pick me up, his tone was very different. I had him right where I wanted him. I played the victim which was easy for me. The monster in me was rising. I wanted him to feel how low I felt. I wanted him to feel pain emotionally. I knew it was wrong, but my thoughts were not set up to make the right choice. I was an adult with an adolescent brain. My whole world was emotional. I couldn't make sense of anything if it wasn't about how I felt. He was the only one that catered to those emotions. We talked about the same incident for days. He still didn't get my point. I wasn't fulfilled. I started flirting more and made more guy friends. I would contact guys from my past, which did nothing for me. I just needed that reminder that I was still important and no one could make me feel less. What my boyfriend didn't know wasn't going to hurt him. I took it too far which woke me up but I was all still playing with fire. I had a guy friend from college that I became very close to. We weren't close sexually. I just like having guy friends over female friends. I met this math tutor on campus that reminded me of my boyfriend in every way. We had so much in common. He was such a breath of fresh air. He was who I turned to when I needed to vent. He was graduating the next day and I wanted to show him that I appreciated him just listening to me. That night some friends and I attended a party and it went too far. I climbed through his dorm window and crashed at his place. I woke up the next morning ashamed of what had happened. For days it was on my mind. I wanted to tell my boyfriend that I cheated, but that would make me just like him. So I kept it in. It was all about me. I wish I could have seen the bigger picture and not retaliate. My boyfriend was my everything. I really wanted to make it work. I went home for break. I didnt think things would go back to the way they were but our relationship got stronger and the sex got hotter. We continued the relationship but he was so far away and I questioned the distance, but

we made it work. The school year was over and summer was just getting started. I *thought* I had contracted something like a sexually
transmitted disease. I was the age of consent at the time so I was happy
I didn't need an adult to take me to the doctor. Last doctor's appointment Queen took me, I got in big trouble because I had a passion mark
on my neck. I definitely couldn't tell her anything. I felt nauseous, weak
and like I had to faint. I kept questioning his loyalty because I was sure
he knew he gave me something. We arrived at the doctor's office to
make sure we both were ok, I was out of it i couldn't stand up. I was so
light headed. The doctor came in with the results. I made him leave the
room because in the back of my mind I could be the blame as well. The
doctor told me the test results came back normal and that I was pregnant. I instantly started to cry. I called him back into the room. I told
him the news and his response wasn't what I thought it would be. He
was concerned. He asked me how I was feeling and did I need anything.
We had to consider all options. This was the scariest day of my life. He
didn't leave my side and that meant a lot because I needed him. Some
days I would stay at my aunt's house rather than return to Queen's
house. My aunt knew before I even told her the news. He did a great
job securing my needs so I knew he would be a great dad. I felt bad
because I didn't want to ruin his life. I knew little to nothing about an
abortion, but I wanted to make him feel like he had a option in it whatever it was. I couldn't believe I had the chance to be someone's mother.
I couldn't possibly be someone's mother when I had things I needed
to get right in my life. I wasn't healed from my past and I didn't want
that in my child's life. I went back to school that Sunday. I couldn't stop
worrying. I decided that I wasn't going to get rid of my child because it
was my love child. At school some of my friends knew and they were
very supportive. I was the only student pregnant. I thought all eyes
were on me . I wasn't that far along. I had a journey to go. I was very
paranoid. I appreciated how everyone respected him even after the
horrible things I said about him out of anger. That made me feel like he
had an amazing girlfriend but in all actuality I was broken. I started to
think the worst in everything once again. I was about three months

pregnant and I finally had the balls to come out to my parents. My dad said he knew because I came home and did not attend church. The secret was out and I was growing by the day. I felt disgusted being pregnant. I tried my best to remain focused in school. It was such a hard thing to do but I didn't give up. I started to attend church more on the weekends I would come home. All the members that were like family to me were shocked. One of the members I looked up to told me how she became pregnant in college. She had to take a year off but she came back to finish. She wasn't me so I couldn't relate. I listened to her story but I wasn't as strong willed as she was. I thought I could keep going but life really sat in for me. All my friends seemed like they were getting their full experience of college and I was just pregnant. I became very depressed and I started to rely on my child's father for everything. My feelings, funds, and even transportation. I know that became alot for him so I decided to commute and get my own apartment so things would work out for us. The state paid for my apartment as well but I had to cover electricity. The amount of responsibility was so draining but i pushed through. My moods started to change and I was afraid again. I was such an angry person towards him. Commuting became overwhelming at eight months. Some days were better than others. I wanted to give up honestly. He was there every step of the way that's why I didn't give up. I honestly owe him the world and more. I couldn't move or sleep as I got closer to my due date. I gained so much weight. I felt ugly . I would pick arguments just because. I know he wanted to leave me. He would stay with me often but I made it about me all the time. How selfish of me. Our relationship wasn't the same. I felt the distance but I knew I still loved him. This man broke a lot of barriers within me and I wanted to know how long he would be in my life. He didn't show his emotions often but one night I wanted to test the limit. We were talking about our future and of course I brought up the past. He randomly asked me If I had cheated on him. I hesitated because I was afraid he would knock my head clean off. He deserved the truth. I told him I cheated while at college. He said he had a gut feeling. He made me repeat the story several times within five minutes to see if I switched up my story. He started to cry. I had never seen a man cry and this was the first time he showed his emotions. He wanted to leave that night but I didn't want him to. He felt my pain and I enjoyed it. I called my aunt for everything. She gave me some very great advice. After the talk if he wanted to leave the door was wide open. He stayed with me and we both cried ourselves to sleep. I knew things would be different. I wanted him hoping that what I told him that night would make our relationship stronger. Instead it got worse. He kept his distance and wanted more and more space. We had a baby shower which was amazing but our relationship just wasn't quite the same. I started to question everything. Was love something i really wanted and deserved? I stopped attending school which was the worst thing I could have ever decided. My lease was about to end and I needed a plan b. I had my first child and didn't know how I was going to take care of her on my own. I put my pride aside and asked my parents to return home. I moved back in with my parents' house. They knew it was hard for me and that I needed them more than anything. I was a new mom with the same scars. My parents helped me adjust to this new life. They allowed my child father to come over anytime he wanted. He just couldn't stay overnight. Their rules were still pretty strict. He didn't like the restrictions, i was used to them. He suggested that we move in with his mother. I was all for us being together as a family. At this time my biological mother and I tried to rekindle our relationship. She was sober and stable at the time. I didn't mind helping my family in any way, especially because we were separated for a long time. I wasn't in a position to help them as much as i wanted to but anything i had they had. I eventually started to look for work just to regain my independence back. Reuniting with my mother didn't heal my wounds at all. I felt she owed it to my daughter to get herself together. I needed her help more than ever. I had a lot to say to her and sometimes the things i said was out of anger. I always yearned for a family. I had the power to reunite my family so i did. I decided to move with my mother and brothers. In my mind I thought my mom would try her best to stay sober, but stressful situations eventually made her relapse. She was under a lot of pressure in that house, I could have made it better for both of us but it was a lot of unsolved feelings just corrupting the energy. My child's father started to distance himself even more because I was back to doing what I knew best which was finding ways to cope with shit. I wasn't sure if we were together or seperated. I became more and more angry with him. I decided to start dating. I wasn't focused at all on what I needed to do. I began to search for things to feel the void again. I seeked the wrong attention. Some days I would leave my daughter home with my mom just to run the streets. I was young and lost, I thought I needed to have fun still. I invited different men into my space. I would talk to different men at a time. I just wanted that security that my ex boyfriend gave me. It wasn't the same. I knew our relationship hit rock bottom when he would come get the baby and leave. He didn't acknowledge me at all. At this point we were over. I tried to get his attention but he knew that other girl in the mirror was coming out that I told him about. He never witnessed her until we broke up. That girl was heartless, cold, angry, manipulative, and damaged. I did everything in my might to make it work, but I became bitter and spiteful. The monster was coming out once again and this time everyone around was getting hit on purpose because I was hurt. I hate that my feelings were dependent on others. I lost the love of my life and everyone needed to feel how I felt. The old me came out but this time alcohol was involved. I would get so drunk and have sex. That became a routine drinking, partying,sex and passing out. When I had my daughter she was my first priority, I changed for her but my pain grew stronger and I couldn't focus on being a mother . I was damaged and drowning in my own sorrow. I couldn't even finish school because I allowed my emotions to take over me, but in a different form this time. Could this be the monster that was deep inside of me? What added to my pain was that I allowed my mother back in my life and we didn't solve the issues from my childhood. I was very disrespectful towards her but I was willing to help my family by all means. In some ways it set me back but in other ways I learned some valuable lessons about pouring from an empty cup. I gave them more than I had just to make sure they were happy. So much time was missing I felt I owed it to them to get it back. I was signed out of the system which meant I was free to run my own life. I wish I would have known I would fall flat on my face. I didn't have control because I didn't know the first thing about really being on my own. I started to feel the distance I created between myself and Queen's family. It didn't happen intentionally, but it happened. I had a heart of gold which kept me grounded. I knew how to make anyone's day brighter. Little things like that made me feel good inside. Just seeing others happy and knowing I had something to do with it. I just couldn't think about me and I despised that about me.

Chapter 12

At this point I wasn't happy and everything around me didn't make sense. I felt the world owed me everything because it took so much away. I was in a confused place. I was in a hurt place and trying to establish a better relationship with my mother, as well as trying to heal from my past made things worse. I knew I had everything inside of me to get it right but, when I took one step forward I took seven steps back. I was even detached from being a mom at a point of time. How could something so precious and harmless deserve this? Then I thought back and saw how I turned out and didn't want her to be anything like I was. I was in the same position my mother was in as a young girl, just trying to deal with life. It was hard for her trying to pull herself together while raising five kids as well as being in love. As a woman we lose ourselves then we find ourselves becoming something we say we never will be. I will admit going through all I did after I had my child helped me realize what I had to lose. I started looking for better job opportunities. I lost a job. I found new jobs. I worked graveyard shifts that I hated. I attempted to get back in school, but then I still didn't have the motivation to finish. I went through so many changes. I wanted to take care of everyone around me, my siblings, my mother, my friends but not me. I disrespected myself, my body and didn't appreciate life. I became homeless, I stayed with queens daughter and sometimes with my child's father. Depending on others while being a mother made me ashamed like I had failed at life. I had never felt this low in my life because I've always felt so high being with the Queen, but I had to find me in the midst of all that I had been through. As my daughter got older I cherished the love she had for me. That really opened my eyes because I couldn't let her down. I was very protective over her. I've always worked hard so that wasn't an issue. The issue became when I put my emotions in charge of my actions. I didn't see my father for years but once I started a new job which was in a prison I finally saw him. He was an inmate. Who knows why I saw him in the state he was in which wasn't a good one. I instantly froze up when i saw him. I hated working in the prison, but I made the best of it. I respected the inmates; they were human. I didn't treat them any less, and they respected me. When I saw my dad a lot of memories came rushing back. He was there for me at a point in my life. I didn't dwell on the past. I needed him but not the way he was. It was like the roles were reversed. He needed me and I was fine with that. That's when I learned God's timing was everything. After all these years I couldn't even tell if he was my dad or not. I didn't envy him as much and I didn't know why I just wanted to make sure he was okay. I put a word in with the inmates I was working with and they took care of him. Since the year 2012 he has been sober. We didn't speak often because I felt he had to regain all that was lost in him. Just seeing him made me want to hug him and tell him I needed him. I needed him to help me understand a lot of things about men and why he wasn't there all these years. I didn't hate him, I just wasn't happy about his decisions in life. I had a child now so a lot of things had to change, but I didn't know where to start. I burnt down bridges and I blocked my blessings. I dug so many holes for my grave and I still managed to want to live for myself. I didn't owe it to anyone but my child. I wanted to become a better version of me for her. Things didn't work out with my mom and I living together. She had things she needed to work on and so did I. I had people around me that still cared but they were ready for me to get my life together. I was ready to heal, but I had to learn to forgive and express what I felt even when I didn't want to. I wanted more out of life than just a job. I had goals I wanted to accomplish. They were just too hard to reach at the time. I wanted to make a difference in others' lives. I wanted people to see that you can have the worst hand dealt to you, but it's all about how you play it. I could have ended up at a facility, a group home, or even a psych ward the way I was acting out, but God knew I was special. He knew I was a warrior. I endured so much and still wanted more out of life. Even though I failed with love I still want to find love. Even though I burned bridges I still want to build genuine relationships from here on out. I had to learn to stop expecting people to treat me how I treat them. I treated people horribly when trying to find myself. Now that I'm older I have learned that healing myself meant that I had to forgive, rebuild, and accept myself first.

I eventually reached out to a mentor at my church because she worked at a mental facility for kids. These kids had all types of problems. Family issues, sexually abused, neglected, just everything that I can relate to. I gravitated towards them . I grew to help them prepare for the real world, I grew to love what I've been through so I wanted them to feel that love. I know it sounds crazy but as I was healing I was still facing the same problems. God sent me the same test until I passed them. This present day I'm still faced with the same tests, but I will say there aren't many of them that I'm struggling with.

These kids loved me. I've gained great rapport with kids and their trauma. Some days I had to refrain from crying because the kids and I had similar traumas. I didn't care how everyone else treated them. I just knew I wasn't going to treat them how everyone else was treating them. This job gave me the strength to save the world. This job also gave me the courage to build a genuine relationship with the world. I looked for a better place to live. I moved into my own place with a roommate. That didn't work out, but I felt I became so nice and noticed I didn't allow the situation to get out of hand. I felt myself growing in better ways but my niceness was taken for granted. I thought because

SOME PLACE TO GROW

I did so much wrong In the past and it was time for change. My daughter was getting a little older. Being a mother made me tough and very assertive. In my mind it was nothing she would lack due to my past. I wanted her to be smart, tough, and able to be a warrior in the cruel world. I felt at times i was too hard on her. She was only a child but in my mind i was preparing her for war. She wasn't ready for that and at times i had to really back down and show her that nurturing and sensitive side i kept hidden. She was so amazing. She was animated,silly,caring and innocent. I often reminisce when my family was together. Him and i made sure this little girl was happy but alone i couldn't give her that. Her dad and I weren't together, and I was unstoppable. Yes, I dated people but it never worked out. I've always attracted guys that hurt me or needed my strength to regain theirs. They couldn't commit. I settled for a lot of this type of behavior because I felt less than. I waited 18 years to be in a real relationship so I knew I had 18 more to go to find another one. I have encountered so many issues just trying to find out who I really was. I thought I was taking the wrong turns. I knew how to discipline myself because the Queen instilled that in me. I tried my best to get back to what I knew. I was in the real world and I was struggling. Things were going well for a while but then minor situations would occur. Bill would be behind, car troubles occurred,and work became overwhelming. All I knew was I was tired of myself. I was tired of failing at life. I had to catch the bus for about 2 years before getting a new car. I hated that process because I felt like I was losing my own race. I had the strength, but I didn't have the direction. I researched everything at this point. That was how I gained my strength to keep going. Just learning new things and keeping myself busy helped me regain structure in my life. I taught myself a lot so why was I incapable of having that same courage? I think I became so reliant on queenie taking care of everything for me. I was an adult but figuring out the way of life was pretty challenging. I used to take cabs to work in the winter which took a lot of my money. I became a regular to this cab driver . The cab driver and I became well acquainted. We had chats during the car rides that were very helpful. He shared with me the amount of money I was spending on fare could equal a monthly car note. I researched it and asked my aunt a thousand questions. Weeks later I purchased my first car in my own name. That made me feel like I could actually start over. It took some time to regain my purpose. I wasn't giving up this time. I started to challenge myself more. I started to push myself in uncomfortable places just to gain knowledge of what I didn't know. Once that happened people around me felt I became big headed. I didn't feel like I was better than anybody. I just felt I owed it to myself to get my life together even if I acted like it was all together. The same amount of energy I had being angry, being jealous, being a liar, being in a place that I've never wanted to be was the same energy I had to use to become the person I needed to be for me and my child. I had to put all of my energy into forgiving, into loving, into positive thoughts, and into positive actions. I wasn't perfect, but I was healing and I could feel it. Just accepting how bad I was hurting helped me put things in categories and sort them out day by day. This process wasn't going to happen overnight but I was sure to take the necessary steps to start somewhere. I wanted my family to be together, but I hurt someone that loved me really badly. I knew if he did return I would have to accept all that I did to him. I owed it to him to watch him heal from the pain I caused him despite what was thrown my way. I was hurting even more watching that he was hurting himself to get back at me. No matter how many losses I took in life I'm not stopping is what I told myself. I was introduced to this word called karma and when I tell you she was the sickest bitch walking. Excuse my language. You would have thought I spit in her face. She got me good, and I had no choice but to take it. It was almost as if I was restrained to a chair and just watching everyone that I did wrong cut any piece of any body part off. All the while screaming I'm sorry. From this day forward I try my hardest to think of the consequences before I do anything I might regret. Karma made me a very sensitive person as well. I second guessed everything as I got older. No matter how much someone may have disliked me, I tried to reason or even understand their side of things. One time my heart told me he was having relations with someone that I knew. So I literally found the girl's boyfriend and had a good time with him. Yes I know it was wrong, but at the time it made me feel better. Once I saw that it didn't work I dropped him and found some more trouble to get in. Trouble was what made me feel relevant. I stopped playing with people when I felt my humanity was gone. He was so fed up with the way I was that he distanced himself from me. I had a shot at love and I messed it all up. I knew I had to really do a 360 because this man did not deserve half the trouble I put him through. No man is perfect, but he was more than my heart he helped me in any and every way. He never told me no. He treated me like the woman I didn't think I deserve to be. He made me feel so comfortable with life that even when I went left he would stay on my right. It wasn't fair to him that I was so damaged. I pray every night that I could be the woman he needs but it's too late. I dreaded to get to this point in my life where all the things I went through were behind me. I wasn't scared to right my wrongs anymore If it meant that I would become a better person or it could give me peace. His family is phenomenal when it comes to my daughter and I wouldn't dare take that away, but just not being his wife after years made me question how much of the past did I let go. It wasn't up to me to decide how fast and when he healed. Some bridges can't be rebuilt in spite of how many people's lives I thought would benefit from it. There were days and nights I felt alone and that felt like I wanted to give up but I had another life depending on me and I couldn't. Some days I will cry hoping for better days but it starts with me. Yes I want a better life for me and my child. Yes I had to work three times harder than anyone else because of the hand I was dealt and didn't play well, but the overall journey then and now was well worth it. Not only did I grow, I evolved into someone I didn't think I could become. I was dead broke before and I never wanted to do that again just depending on somebody while having a child is the craziest feeling ever. I became my aunt. The matriarch of the family, someone that everybody depends on and someone that everyone goes to. But once again I couldn't pour from an empty cup which I always did. I had to go harder. I wanted more. I always dug myself 100 feet under by helping the people around me. So in order to come back and get everyone I love I have to get where I need to be first. At times I felt I couldn't get through the door because everyone was pulling at my legs. Most of the time I put everyone's needs before mine just to feel like someone needed me. I started to appreciate little things again because I was without a lot. I started taking my time on everything because I was tired of getting hurt. I started to distance myself from a lot of stuff that I used to take my mind off of things: partying, drinking, toxic friends, bad influences, and even greedy family members.

I blame myself at times because wearing your emotions on your shoulders allows people to pick which ones they wanted to play on, on any given day. I started to work a lot. I started to do more things I loved doing. More writing, more me time, more spending time with my child. I even started working on how I respond and how to not react so quickly. I attended Church more and listened to sermons. I would even cry in church because the Pastor was literally talking about me. I felt like at this point I was yearning to heal myself. I didn't want to not have a handle on emotions anymore. I didn't want to have sleepless nights. I didn't want to have weary days. I wanted to be free. I wanted to love me. I stopped giving so much of myself to the world and started giving myself more to God. Once again I'm not perfect but my walk is different. My body went through so much stress and before it was too late changes in my body took over. I woke up one morning with pain in my hands and my knees and I didn't know what to do. Something wasn't right and i had no one to call but my mother. I cried profusely. I had to num the pain for the moment until I could take time to schedule an appointment. Eventually I went to the doctor because it was unbearable and they told me I had rheumatoid arthritis. I went for a second opinion and they diagnosed me with lupus. I just knew i was going to die soon. I was on medication for a year which stopped the pain but weakened my immune system. I thought I was going to die but it wasn't my choice and it wasn't a doctor's choice. It was God's choice. Even though the pain I knew I had to take necessary steps to stay healthy

. I didn't want my body to go through anything that brought stress to it. I decided that I wouldn't take the medication anymore. I always had a weak immune system, but this time I thought it was at an all-time low. I started to research what they diagnosed me with and how the medicine would affect my body. I went to a second doctor and she told me all I had to do was convert to a more healthy way of living. I didn't like vegetables because we ate so much as a kid and I wasn't giving up meat. I stopped being stubborn and I eventually changed my diet about six months in. I started losing so much weight but I started feeling energized and amazing. I started feeling less pain so I knew whatever the doctor told me the first time could possibly be true. This is how they made their money and I wasn't mad. I just knew the decision I made changing my diet helped me for the better. I stayed on top of my health. I went once again to make sure i was alright and the ruled out the lupus factors. I was relieved because I researched it and it gave me death scares. I had so much life to live and so much work to do that i couldn't possible die early.

Chapter 13

It's so weird how things tie into one another as life happens for me. I used to believe I was like this chosen one many times in my life because each lesson I learned made the hurt I felt decrease. When I say I have been through the mud and came out squeaky clean please believe it. God could have given me superpowers, but instead he kept them on hold for me. I learned what my superpower was as I began to allow people to actually help me. Being in a system where all types of workers or lawyers or judges had more control over my life than my own parents, I had many doubts that things wouldn't change for me. I will admit that when I was placed in my final foster home things started to look up for me. During the challenging times of being in foster care I had doubts at first but they began to fade away once I started to accomplish major accomplishments that others saw I was capable of. I started to believe there was hope for me. The downfall to that was when I did accomplish milestones in my life I saw them as something small. My insecurities played a huge part in the way I observed things and how I responded to them as well. I learned that if I thought negatively then I would see negative and do negative. It was hard for me to convert this way of thinking. As I entered adulthood I saw that everyone around me was so confident and motivated to become better and make a great life for themselves. Whatever they were drinking I wanted some. It was very hard not feeling one hundred percent supported or motivated. It took me many times to understand that being uncomfortable didn't mean it was the end of the world. The fact that I was so uncomfortable in my life made me go harder. God took me through the toughest obstacles which taught me forgiveness and strength. I started not to care about what was around me but more so what was in me. Some days I felt I didn't have anything to live for because I didn't know my purpose in life. I didn't know who I really was or what I wanted to be in life. The added trauma I faced made life twice as hard for me. During my trauma period which was around my teenage years I used to think I was invincible. Every wall I came across couldn't stand taller than me. The wall had to be knocked down because I couldn't see through it. I wanted everything to be clear and overt. I felt if I couldn't see through it then it wasn't real, but what did I know about real? I made up stories in my head to paint a picture that wasn't there to hide behind my truth. At times my insecurities had me afraid of trying new things. It was so weird because as bad as I was afraid to try new things in my life during the "who am I" stage which was adulthood I would get into new trouble and I wasn't afraid of the consequences behind it. I feared change because I couldn't see the outcome for myself in the midst of my hurt. I feel I limit myself today because of ignorance from my past. Me not knowing that it was light at the end of every tunnel kept me in a place of helplessness. Growing up, my hope was lost. I wish I was that kid that went through trauma and used it to become something like an astronaut. I thought nothing would ever go as planned. Entering the system haunted me for a very long time, but with the help of God I got through it. My thought process had me in the toughest situations that no human can bear. The system was very quick to diagnose kids with a mental illness due to how they reacted to trauma. I didn't want someone telling me what they thought was wrong with me. They put my brothers on medication but I knew that wouldnt cure their pain. I knew deep inside that the system would make you or break you because some people can't handle being out of their comfort zone. The most amazing thing about the situation was when I came out of the disasters I created for myself I was clean. Clean meaning innocent. I was already emotionally destroyed so I didn't feel anything. The fact that I learned from my mistakes made me do better. I knew some of my actions weren't fair or the right thing to do, but I wanted everything I thought I was missing inside. It almost felt like I was on a battlefield of lessons I needed to learn from in order to grow, but I didn't understand that until I was in my mid 20s. Well I won't just give you the ending because it's not over yet, I'm still healing and trying to hide the scars of my past. I will admit if you really know me you know I don't look like what I've been through and by the grace of God I pray I continue to find some place to grow. I'm actually still being faced with some tough decisions in life today that require me to think logically and spiritually first. I feel honored because I finally have that option to think rationally. I've grown to understand that you have a choice in everything you do. But I will tell you a secret, when you are able to think logically and have peaceful thoughts it makes handling life's problems so much more worth it. As I'm writing this book I've had several negative thoughts. It made me second guess myself, like do I really want people to know who I really am and do I really want them to know what I went through. On the other hand I want them to understand and explain the behaviors from my past. A lot of people really are confused like here we have this generous female with a big heart, but she didn't care how her actions affected others.

Side note while writing this I'm not embarrassed at all. I feel very confident in whatever you all read and lastly, I am happy. Being happy was always my goal until I was happy and still needed more. I wanted peace. Peace for my mind and my thoughts and a chance to be born again. Being born again for me was accepting my actions as well as changing them from here on out. Admitting to myself that what I may have done wasn't right and it was an act of hurt. Lastly repenting to the man upstairs and apologizing to the people I may have hit with my storm. After that stage in my life a lot of situations were easy to handle. I allowed very few to reopen my wounds but I didn't let them take over or destroy me. A lot of times if I did anything out of emotion to get back at someone I instantly had to make it right. My thought process became very positive. I started to see the beauty in everything and everyone. Oftentimes I was too numb to retaliate but when I did it was bad. I had to stop the madness because everyone started to disappear. I had to learn to stop worrying about what people did to me but how I responded. Everyone didn't have my best interests at heart and I wanted God to remove them because I became weak to peer pressure. I wanted to become a better person, but I didn't know how. I went back to what I knew and that was talking to God as well as attending church. I loved my Pastor because he wouldn't just preach, he would also teach us how to follow God. I began to use his sermons and apply them to the areas in my life where I needed them. A weight lifted off my shoulders because I wanted the better version of me. Even though I burned a lot of bridges I was a master swimmer, and I was able to cross the bridge to apologize to anyone I affected. I also developed this thing where I had a plan b for everything just in case something doesn't work out. Going through life put my body and mind through so much wear and tear that I neglected to take care of myself. I needed therapeutic outlets. I started to write more of my thoughts down. I started to share and listen to what others were going through. I started to help in the community and even take time for myself. I knew it was time to take care of me. I had a child that needed a healthy, mentally stable role model. I had the courage to share my story when I was told how much people looked up to me. I had no choice but to share what I had been through to become the person I am today.

Have you ever made choices in life, dreaded the consequences but actually learned from it? Well I have! I never thought I could be in touch with my emotions. I never thought I separated what I was taught and what protected me for years from what I thought was right. It's so weird because i couldn't see B feelings but looking back she saved me from death. Her teachings stuck with me, even though I was far out of my league at times. Just going back to what she practiced saved me in a lot of situations. It's so easy to do the wrong thing and not having that strength to do the right thing makes any situation ten times worse. Til this day i'm comfortable and happy that i try my best not to be of this world. I'm content and love my originality and genuine ways. I am actually able to face the girl in the mirror which was an accomplishment I deeply cherish in my life. That girl in the mirror was vicious when I saw what she was capable of. I became an angry, sad, and lonely girl at a point of time because I was so complacent to what I thought my path was. I did not allow anyone to show me that it was more to life than my situation. I wanted to fix what was broken by any means. Growing up I fought against the reality of a lot of situations. I didn't want to face the reality of my life. Many times I would fantasize about what I wanted my life to be instead of accepting what it is. The sad part was I wasn't able to say I wanted to be at peace with myself and my thoughts because pain felt natural. I will admit accepting your own shit is very hard when you care about what others think of you. Not knowing myself allowed people to use me in crazy ways. I actually became someone else due to the lack of care

I had built up inside. I was damaged and I needed to figure out who I was. I was shaped to think emotionally in everything I did. I had no logic bone in my body. My thoughts were emotional, my lifestyle was emotional, my dreams were emotional, my nightmares and my reactions became emotional. Every reaction was off impulse. I was always in this flight or fight phase. Growing up I didn't grasp the fact that I could grow in the midst of my sorrow and pain. Life took me on one hell of a ride. I felt every bump, breakdown, and detour you could imagine. I thought I could get through the hurt, but I actually became hurt along the way. Many instances I strongly thought I let go of my past but it was attached to me. I thought I grew through it mentally but I only grew physically. I was faced with the same situations just disguised in different forms. As I got older I was capable of accepting it all. When I was younger, learning from my mistakes made me upset. I wasn't mature enough to the point that I could see that my actions were a cry for help. I blamed everyone around me for my own personal life. For me mistakes were plural. I literally looked for different mistakes to make just to find different results. I learned the definition of insanity at a very young age. The world owed me a new life and I was going to get it one way or another. It had gotten so bad that I seeked revenge on myself because I allowed my feelings to overtake me. I didn't understand that I had the power to control my next move. It had gotten so bad I was drowning in my own sorrow. Being a great swimmer didn't help one bit. I burned so many bridges that in order to regain those relationships I would have to prove to the people I loved that my soul was pure and the real me just wanted to be wrapped in the arms of people that said they loved me. After the many challenges, I faced enough was enough, I sat down with myself and swallowed the pill. I allowed my trauma to define me which led to my actions and choices I made in my life. That was the only way to use what I knew. I began to read the bible. I read the entire chapter of revelations. That chapter left me in trembles. I knew that I didn't want to die in pain. I wanted to heal and live at the same time. I knew that I had to make a choice. It was hard getting back on the right path when I would put the world first. I was of the world by my actions but I felt I was different. Many of the mistakes I made and the people I hurt were just as beneficial. I didn't mind helping anyone out. I pulled every limb of my body just to make others happy. I began to talk to God when I didn't have the answers. I attended church frequently but I still didn't listen. Years later after fighting myself and my past I started to eliminate things that stopped me from growing like friends, partying, sex, drugs, and alcohol. I realized that every time I fell into a dark place I would turn to those things instead of turning to God. A lot of my mistakes became repetitive over time and not only was everyone tired of it, so was I. Only thing I was sure of was that I knew that God had got me out of many situations even if I couldn't physically see him. Trusting someone that you couldn't see was the challenging part for me. I wanted to see this person's face that got me out of the hole I was putting myself in. I would slide back from his word but return in wholeheartedness. I had days where I would question him, but of course I didn't listen and fell straight on my face. I struggled a lot with my insecurities growing up. I asked for love and popularity, but when God gave me those things I wasn't in the right state of mind so I abused them horribly. I made a bad name for myself and all because I wanted love and to be known. When I had those things I didn't want them anymore because it got old. I wanted more of myself. I grew to understand and follow his word. For me, being a Christian had many stipulations but I saw it as doing good in a world full of evil. I wanted to treat people how I liked to be treated. I still had angry tendencies but grew to communicate how I was feeling. I stopped projecting my wrong opinions on others and started to educate myself. God always gave me things to compare my life to. He made me realize that things that are good don't always grow in the most beautiful places. I look at it like vegetables are in the dark wet ground for months in order to provide you with the best nutrients. The only way I was going to be of any good in this world was if I did good. My mind shifted into another level that I never experienced. I realized that it was never once about me. God wanted to use me as a testimony. I am not perfect is what I remind people, but God purposely made my heart pure. As I continued to find places to grow all the dead toxins fell off. God was right there on my shoulder letting me know there is a choice in every decision you make. I gained strength though my journey as well as self love. I had days where certain words like mother or father or even home made me emotional. God gave me something better and that was a security blanket which was made out of his love if I wanted to stay wrapped in it. That blanket has kept me safe and warm and worry free ever since. If I had any advice to give every human being walking this earth it would simply be live life like it's no tomorrow, love freely, forgive openly, wish for the best, but expect the worst, perform multiple acts of kindness daily and lend a helping hand. Do not become of this world and a sound mind you will have. In exchange for my peace I became a better me as well as a better mother and friend to those around me. I'm not perfect but I have a pure heart that was on fire for quite some time. I honestly want to take the time to truly apologize to any and everyone that was affected by my trauma. Can't wait for you to meet the healed me.

Who am I? Does anyone really sit and ask themselves that question? Well, I'll be the first to admit I've asked myself this question over and over again and got no answer. Funny how you are here on this earth and have no clue of your own existence. Don't feel bad. It took me years to figure it out. Til this day I'm still learning myself, but the only difference is now I'm falling in love with the journey of completing me. I wrote my first poem and who knew I was so close to figuring out my world. The title was called Who am I? I was searching hard for myself, Perfect age to explore and the perfect age to be curious as well. At that time I had no clue what I was writing about. I was just putting words together and different challenges others faced around me or even my own feelings in one poem.

All the complications erupted in my life and were predestined. I had no choice but to go through all I went through . What I've been through and how far I've come has been my biggest motivating source to keep fighting to reach my full potential and purpose of who I am. The battle of finding me was no easy task, but what task is? I fought three people for years: who I was born into, who I became, and who I was destined to be. It became less of a fight once I reached who I was destined to be because I got rid of old habits and started doing things right. It was more of a victory. The victory was my peace, my sound mind, and my ability to think logically in everything. Sounds small right? But knowing these things made a difference in my life. These small things were all I needed to sleep at night. Knowing I did my best to make my soul laugh, my heart love, lend a helping hand, and even being a genuine individual made me love harder and let go of things that no longer served me. Let's rewind it from the beginning. God always had a bigger plan for my life but if I didn't believe it or see it the plan didn't exist. Before it existed I had to go through the highs and lows. I became a lost soul just yearning for wholeness within myself but expected it from everyone else because I thought the world owed me what was taken away at a very young age. I added family, friends, and even strangers into my tragedies. Some hurt me and some helped me along the way. I thought I lost so much and losing gave me more of a reason to fight so hard towards a better me but in the midst of it, I lost me. Who knew that rain makes things grow, and who knew that flowers can grow through concrete?

Poems

1. As a father, this is the life you choose and as your kids, we look up to you whether you win or lose. We never question the investment, sacrifice, energy, and time spent to make sure you're there as our father, but I'm pretty sure we see your hard work and dedication to meet the goal. That's true motivation to me as your child. To see that you put everything you've been through aside so it doesn't interfere with your role. Your tired days are handled so effortlessly and yet I've never seen you fold. Happy Father's Day to you

2. I sleep alone every night wondering why you're not by my side. I look at the shadows and get scared, calling your name like you are there. I create our memories on the wall but my cries as comfort won't leave me alone. Everything I didn't know I experienced with you. My pain wasn't your fault but that's how I grew. You stuck by my side and that's how I knew. I knew what becomes of love, what a daddy was, what I had could be lost, and why I had to fight against all odds. I stole your time and made it my own. My burning heart couldn't be cooled by your waters. And I still hold back when I'm in your presence because your unknowingly thoughts pierce my soul. I wish I could fix every emotion I abused and use

them for someone like you. Time may not be on my side but the love still remains. My heart may not be on fire anymore but your chill waters are still in my veins

3. Expectations

I wanted you to teach me and Learn me until our hearts start letting go then touch me and assure me that we would hold on until we both started to seeing growth. Do you know who my father is so protection, love, and faith wouldn't be an issue. I was different. I was giving you balance, but it wasn't something you seemed to be into. you said you were afraid of me well shit I was afraid of me too. I took the time to heal myself from all the hurtful things I've been through. Does that make me a savior? Does that not sound pretty extraordinary to you? I bet it doesn't,and to think I considered all he noise and the commotion you deal with each and every day. I wanted to help you deal with all that so I could get the sound minded you, and I still wanted to be your warmth and happiness that people forget to leave when they walk another way. Standing back not giving you too much of me just to see if you were this game lost boys love to play. Still haven't quite figured out why you scream you're free when clearly you're drowning and all you need is your heart to be saved.

4. I hate feeling alone or feeling blue. I gave my heart to a man that could care less about two. I shut my mouth to avoid arguments or debates that go south. I spent years trying to fix things that I thought would work out. I stayed loyal to my morals and values which lead me to you, but in fact I met a heartless individual that could care less about two. Selfish to love and ignorant to evolution, influenced by many situations of toxic pollution. Emotionally wired differently and his pride was the worst. I pray for a button to pop up that says " reverse". Have you ever been filled with swallowed anger? So clogged you could burst. Or been so turned

off by things that didn't hold any worth.

5. I want to feel how I felt when I first laid eyes on you. I want that adrenaline in my body that no one can take away only you. I want that feeling when I close my eyes and grip my body I think of you. Heavy breathing I use as a fan when we face one another as we sleep. I want that I'm worried, but you'll grab my face and kiss my lips purifying my soul. I want that whenever I fall you'll be there to laugh then help me up. I want that I hate your guts but love your butt type feeling. I want to keep my distance from you for at least a minute and that will be too long. I want to feel how I felt when we made endless love and I was so out of breath. The feeling of change just makes me regret what I had no control over. . .The feeling of love just makes me reminisce about you.

6. Press reset

Knowing you can't do anything physical due to the pain and urge you feel inside. You have no choice but to let the man that died for you handle all your problems. Sounds weak right? I thought so at first but I was wired differently. I knew that my painless peaceful day would come very soon. Every day we act off emotions or the urges of revenge and hurt and we never see the bigger picture. You would be the same if you retaliated or even questioned God. So I sat and played it over and over in my head and on one hand I thought about doing what every mad black woman would do but on the other hand, I thought about what God would do. And as the tears rolled down my face I realized no matter how much someone says they love you, loving yourself and where God has brought you from is all that matters. Despite the pain, you feel because he didn't say it wouldn't be painful but he reassured you that he would never leave us nor forsake us and that's how you feel the relief of pain. remembering you have a legacy and goals to accomplish and not being of the world.

7. I'm thankful for the energy I may have to restore

Because when God gives you less it really means more

I'm thankful for new opportunities and fresh starts

Not for what I gained but what I lost

I'm thankful for togetherness, Humbleness, and peace within.

But most of all I'm thankful for being able to say I can help you, my friend.

I'm thankful for my morals and values that keep me full.

And the biggest one of all is my own testimony to motivate the unsure

I'm thankful for constant change and the ability to live my most precious life

But most of all being able to say my prayers with my little girl every night.

Then I was thankful for the clothes on my back and the shoes on my feet

Now I'm thankful for being able to give to every homeless person I see.

When I was younger I was thankful for the food that I eat

but now that I'm older I'm thankful for more greens and less meat.

I'm thankful for my strength and passion to become the best me

but as we know thanksgiving then and now is all about evolution and growth for me.

8. She so much like me

She's so much like me I mean like a reflection in the mirror,

I couldn't say it any clearer.

Down to the extra silly behavior or the mood swings which save her. She so much like me

so I laugh to keep from crying or hug her when I feel like I'm dying. From the little white lies, she uses as protection or the mouthy feedback I get in one direction…

she's so affectionate it's like she knows I need it and she's so help-ful like you wouldn't believe it.

I see everything in her that many would see in me.

I understand how she feels so I'm at ease with all her choices,

she's only 4 and she doesn't even budge by my intimidating noises.

Yelling of course she makes these crazy faces like mom stop acting like you need personal spaces.

We are so much alike, it's a curse and a blessing at the same time.

I would lose it if it was the end of my lifeline and I didn't see her crazy faces, letting me know that one would ever replace me.

9. All shattered

I'm flattered you think of me as this beautiful girl with remark-able features. I'm also shattered from the past hurt of a woman that was equally and utterly weak as I was. I'm flattered that you think I have genuine ways that make it easy to trust me as a friend but I'm shattered from all of the people that left me in the wind. I'm flattered that you think if you leave me I wouldn't grow. But

I'm shattered from the fact that the relationships I've made lasted two point five seconds i let go. I'm flattered that I could make your body feel good due to my nonchalant lack of emotions but I'm shattered that the one that loved me and made love to me is drowning in the unfair ocean. I'm flattered that you put me in this high caliber but what's more shattering is I'm living in this world with a battered heart. I'm flattered that you think I'm a tough pill to swallow, But I suggest you read and follow the manual that comes with me ahead of time.

10. Old Times

There is a time for sorrow

There is a time for pain

There is a time for weakness

There is a time for gain

There is a time I need you but I want to be alone.

There is a time I breathe you but in fact, you are just a moan.

There is a time I wish and prayed you would make me strong, or hold my hand,

there is a time you acted like a little boy but you really are a man.

There is a time I'm happy again because you are near me.

But then there is a time I cry myself to sleep and you never hear me.

I want it to be a time we both want each other yet again,

so when we have our timeless babies they will see that we both win

I need that time again

11. No phones allowed

I looked through your phone and boy was I hurt.

You had options to choose from but I wasn't her.

you told me you were focusing on yourself but that was very covert.

I made myself available to you cause I thought it would work.

I was wrong to go in it but I was blinded by the words

We scarred one another bad and now what it seems isn't what it's worth

I protected my heart just because I knew for sure that you would come back to get it

but when I looked through that phone my heart went cold.

You talk to them females as if they were queens and the Shit you dish out to me was just so mean

You Were two totally different people which makes it seems that everything you told me was just a scene.

I was afraid of what was out there so I kept our love a secret

I had the man of my dreams but I just couldn't keep it

Mother fuck me No mother fuck you for being so selfish to keep me around for your available convenience.

But this time I'm not playing you're making your own bed and I mean it

12. On cloud nine

Shorty with the clouds Have a big head

But shorty with the clouds do shed tears

Shorty with the clouds look really soft and fluffy but shorty with
the clouds got walls up so don't touch me

Shorty with the clouds sometimes stand-alone but shorty with
the clouds can stand on her own

Shorty with the clouds be in LaLa land

But shorty with the clouds seems to be your biggest fan

Shorty with the clouds is so unpredictable but shorty with the
clouds won't tell you her next move

Shorty with the clouds thinks she's above everyone but shorty
with the clouds can uplift anyone

Shorty with the clouds is up here for a reason but shorty with the
clouds had to go through many seasons

Shorty with the clouds worked hard to stay up so don't get it
twisted

Shorty with the clouds isn't at all stuck.

13. Cupid

I played with love

I mishandled that shit

I acted on impulse and didn't care who got hit.

I was into making myself feel better that I didn't care who didn't fit.

Everyone around me was the least of my concerns.

It had gotten so bad that I was the fire and the burn.

I started losing the people I cared for.

I started feeling alone in the rarest form.

The worst weapon became karma. I literally had to sit and take each punch from everyone I hurt.

the world has to understand one thing about me.

when I feel I have no one I turn to the only things that needed me and that was my weakness.

as I take this withdrawal process to reach my Peak

I sat and felt all pain that I arranged

And yes it got worse the support was gone, the respect disappeared and all the motivation was in use.

I had abused my life.

Then life happened again and I cried because I missed all the bridges I had burnt... and yes there were lessons I did learn

my life was no longer a bad concern

I wanted to fix it, fix it all. . . . but it was too late all love was lost.

I still had my heart and my faith. That kept me straight. The moral of the story you can not play with love and you can't stop living the life you love. IM SORRY made a big mistake

14. Collision

I ran smash into you with fears and doubts.

I hid laughs and love in my closet and you bought that out.

I try to hide the fact that the past has me so hurt inside but every time I'm with you those feelings seem to subside.

I get so serious because I'm afraid you may slip away.

But every joke you make lets me know it's the heart-field way.

Our time together is always filled with fun.

I will never forget that time it was pouring and I made you run.

I promised myself that it will be the last time we disagree or fuss.

because at that moment I realized it's more than just lust.

I'm here to show you that life is not just about

giving, it's receiving, loving, securing, and winning.

I'm still adjusting to how amazing you treat me, but I assure you if you give me some time I'll be yours completely.

The little things you do makes me want you more and more

and if you show me loyalty I'll show that I'm riding for you for sure

15. Scum

I really wish things were different.

I really wish you could the beauty from my eyes of our genuine friendship

I wish you could really see us but you were against it.

Everything I said to you, you took it so offensive

And when you told me to leave you really meant it

Why do things grow when they are so distant?

And why did you start this if you weren't going to finish?

And why would you have me open up to you if you weren't going to let me in

I have so many questions as to why you let it go

But I came up with my own analogy to help me grow.

Guess I had to deal with the cruddiest of them all so I would see my worth and never ever fall.

16. Passenger

I sat back and let you wine and dine me and waste my time with the ultimate goal of screwing me. It's like I pressed forward in my mind without the strength of even trying and now I'm at the part where you ruined me. you played my words against my thoughts leaving my heart to jump in and now I'm in a pool of scrutiny, Leaving me all confused because you had nothing to lose and now It's a battle between you and me. You saw that I was falling with no intention of catching me so instead I caught my own fall and now I'm crawling to you. Feels so weak to be this low but I'm thinking it's helping him grow but instead it's creating a cycle of foolery. How could a good heart be so vulnerable to a weak-minded individual?Now you got me questioning my strengths because I've accepted all your fucked your ways that I thought were undoable.

17. It's not me it's you

It all makes *sense now*

I know why you entered my life. You needed to make a woman out of me

but not make me your wife.

You needed to build me up

Then break me down

so I wouldn't be afraid of heights. You needed to teach me patience but in the same sense

have me waiting to wonder where the fuck you are at night. You needed to wine and dine me and bump and grind me

so I wouldn't think twice about the hype

You needed me to see that

you were just as broken as I was that's why all we do is disagree on life

you needed me to accept your shit to see if the glove would fit

So that your darkness came to light

You wanted to test the waters and break down borders to see if I was worth the fight

And I was willing to give it all up for you just to lay with you every night,

holding you praying for you telling you I loved you

despite all the bullshit we ignite.

But that wasn't enough, your appetite was larger than life.

Realizing you weren't afraid of what could go wrong but knowing in your heart that you didn't want it to go right.

18. Adjust your crown

Mother, I love you

Daughter, I love you too

No mother, you help me, encourage me, support me, and teach me.

No daughter I guide you, protect you and prepare you for the world.

Mother, I follow your lead

No daughter, we are a team.

But mother I watch you bleed

No daughter it's not what it seems

I may stumble or lean but that's just a little reminder that I have to keep pushing for you and me. Mother thank you for all you do,

No thank God he helps us too

19. Makeover

I never met anything like you so I'm intrigued by your presence

the sight and touch of you leave chills down my body that no one could measure

The way you look at me pierce my soul so I know you're learning me. One minute we're on chills than the next minute you're burning me

Helping me separate emotions from logic so things would be easier to find. It's almost like I'm intimidated by your dominant so submissive I'll be. I feel protected even when I'm not around you . Now that's real security. I trust that you see I'm not like anyone else because I'm giving you the real me and even if we don't work out, trust me a woman you'll make of me. Challenging me to see what I thought was good for me only left me behind.

20. The End

I was that comfort for you and I told you, you were that comfort for me.

somehow lines got tied and your understanding of things did not quite reach me.

I got so wrapped up in your words I ignored your thoughts.

I was in a rush to get what I wanted, that I was blinded by what we had and not by what could be lost.

I was so quick to gather all of you without learning your ways, or learning what you do' and don't like so that I can better your days.

I made it about me and I can admit that I was wrong. I forgot to ask if you were alright, how were you feeling inside, or even did you need me to sing you a love song.

I don't want to give up on our chemistry because you just can't make that stuff up.

I pray you to put your pride aside and really forgive me because I'm the reason that wall is back up. what we started seemed half full but now I feel half empty.

You were more than just my Cupid, you were my hopeless romantic ending.

21. Humble

It's the difference between penny-pinching and good living.

I played the victim by spending money on numbing feelings.

My guilty conscience was fighting me instead of demons.

This race of healing has been taking longer than I expected

And every time I push forward I get rejected.

I say lord keep me humble and keep me fed rather than keeping me focused on the things better left unsaid.

22. Let us Pray

I used to say I was thankful for the food that I eat but now I say I'm thankful for more greens and less meat.

I used to say I'm thankful for the shoes on my feet but now now I say I'm thankful for having money to give to every homeless person I see.

I used to say I'm thankful for clothes on my back but not I say I'm thankful for being in a position to give back.

I used to say I'm thankful for being pretty but now I say thanks for having a pretty heart. I used to say I'm thankful for making mistakes but now I'm thankful for new opportunities and fresh starts.

I used to say I'm thankful for togetherness but now I say I'm thankful for the energy I may have to restore.

I used to say I'm thankful for humbleness but now I know whenever god gives you less it really means more. I use to say I'm thankful for my friends but now I say I the full of peace within

I use to be so excited for this one day every year of thanksgiving but now I pray for every single day of the year that I'm living with family and friends now I'm thankful for relationships I may have to make amends

23. SO LONG

We've been through hell and back

We've separated fiction from facts

We sat back and laughed at the old you and I, and then celebrated the new us.

We corrected our mistakes, but then we both got too strong.

You chose the strong image in someone else's eye.

I chose the strong me myself and I.

We tried again, but went through hell and back. We fought our way through trying to make sense of it all. .

You fake the funk, but I smelled right through your stinch. We find our way through hell and back only this time I caught the train and you're still on the track.

24. Man up

You say you don't want me, but you want my front-row seat open for you.

You say you're tired of the fighting, but they ain't going to keep hope as I do.

You say you want to be free, well there's the door let me open it for you.

You say this is too much, but I hold more boulders than you.

You say well you did things too, well my emotions are thing one and your actions are thing two.

You say I don't love them hoes, they come and they go.

Well I say if You throw a stick and I catch it then, you throw a rock and I fetch it.

that would be one hell of a message so please shut my damn door.

25. No Deal

It's really cute how we exchange numbers knowing good well both our minds had wonders.

Right now I'm in a messed up state, But honey please don't make the number one mistake.

For your own sake don't think I'm just some bait, I will change your whole world. My sex will take you to paradise just some sexy advice.

My intellect will make you an emotional wreck. My loyalty to you will be on deck.

That will be your loss if you mess this up.

That will be your loss if your blue balls don't erupt.

I don't want to kill you softly with the addicting ways I want to be the girl that weighs.

Weigh on your heart, your mind, your soul, and your stay. If you want we can do it together no rush just real no lust all-steel fuck up no deal.

You have my attention lips sealed

26. Joker

Time was beneath us but we didnt fall. You seemed to be distant but you weren't far. Butterflies and moths were what you gave me, Your charm and your laugh was what saved me. I was warm around you even though i was freezing inside. You gave me that keep fighting feeling when i wanted to cry. Seconds, minutes, hours stood still with you and i didnt question why. Reality kicked in and time started to fly.

CPSIA information can be obtained
at www.ICGtesting.com
Printed in the USA
LVHW040321290322
714677LV00007B/486

9 781977 228420